I0665500

I WISH
I Woulda Knew Me
BACK THEN
ANTHOLOGY

I WISH
I Woulda Knew Me
BACK THEN
ANTHOLOGY

Compiled by Danielle Green

Copyright ©2014 by Image Publishings
First Edition

ISBN-13: 978-0692228838

1951 Laurel Oak Dr.
Flint MI 48507
www.imagepublishings.com
danielleygreen@yahoo.com

All rights reserved. No part of this book may be
reproduced in any form or by any means including
electronic, mechanical or photocopying or stored in
a retrieval system without prior written permission
from the publisher, except for the inclusion of brief
quotations in a review.

Publisher's Note: Names have been changed to
protect confidentiality. Any similarity to people
living or dead is purely coincidental.

Printed in the United States of America

Cover Design by www.aftertheink.com

Edited by Eagle Eye Editing and Proofreading
Services

DEDICATION

To young ladies everywhere
on their path to discovering who they are

ACKNOWLEDGEMENTS

First and foremost, I want to thank God for His guidance and mercy throughout this journey. Without you, nothing I do would be possible.

Just like most mothers, my babies mean the world to me. Tia, Alyssa and Makala, I LOVE YOU. Everything I do, I do for you.

To the love of my life, Mr. Marvin Johnson, thank you so much for supporting me and believing in me when my life was full of doubters. I LOVE YOU.

To my mother Denise Green and my father Gene Presley, you both have encouraged me to never give up and to never let my situation or circumstances limit my abilities.

To all you ladies, I can't thank you enough for trusting me with your personal, private experiences. My hope is that each and every one of you feel a sense of relief, accomplishment and fulfillment for being a part of this project. Without you opening up and sharing, I could not have fulfilled this dream.

Danielle Ward, I've been trying to think of the words to express to you how much you mean to me. So here it goes. In life we meet all kinds of people, but I have never met anyone who is so sweet, so kind and so giving. Meeting you and having you in my life lets me know that I am being rewarded for doing something right. From the very beginning, you believed in my vision, you supported my vision and you encouraged me to stay true to my vision no matter what. THANK YOU, THANK YOU, THANK YOU.

Special thanks to Michael E. Reid, aka Just Mike the Poet, for allowing me to use your poem. I appreciate you!

TABLE OF CONTENTS

TABLE OF CONTENTS

INTRODUCTION

Early one morning, I awoke from a dream. The dream revealed to me my next assignment. You see, I believe that in life, God gives us all assignments of the heart, and this is one of mine. I envisioned women, including myself, would come together and share a story about a time or situation in our lives, where, if given the opportunity to go back and have a conversation with our younger selves, we would share our lessons learned.

From this, *I Wish I Woulda Knew Me Back Then* was born. One of my passions is to nurture the success of young ladies, and I knew this anthology would allow me to extend my reach beyond my own community and touch the lives of young women everywhere.

The women who contributed to this anthology were willing to dig deep and share their deepest, darkest secrets, regrets and failures. By writing, not only did some of these ladies begin their own healing process, but they opened the door for many of you to do the same.

The purpose of this anthology is to help, teach, encourage, uplift and motivate you as you are on your life's journey. At the end of each story are pages to record your thoughts and feelings.

Danielle Green

Tanya Baker

Tanya Baker was born and raised in Flint, Michigan by her grandparents, Mr. Willie and Mrs. Magnolia Alexander. Mother of two sons, Devante and Gavin, and a daughter-in-law, Porsha, Tanya also has three grandkids: Devante Jr., Denayah, and Komariah.

Ms. Baker returned to school to earn her GED, and then furthered her education at PSI Institute, studying data entry. Afterward, she attended Genesee CNA Academy, training to become a phlebotomy technician, patient care technician and EKG technician. Tanya also went to Mott Community College for Psychotropic Medications, Gastrointestinal Disorders, Urinary System, and Psychotic Disorders.

Later, Tanya received a two-year associate degree as a licensed chef from the Dorsey School of Culinary Arts. She is currently in the planning stages of opening her own catering company.

Ms. Baker would like to give thanks to her sister DeShawndra Hill (R.I.H.) for encouraging her to go back to school and further her education. She would additionally like to thank her cousin Danielle Green for asking her to participate in this journey with her.

FEELING UNLOVED & UNWANTED
Tanya Baker

I was three years old when I started feeling unloved and unwanted. This was when my mother decided that she no longer wanted to be a part- or full-time mother. She was very young, but as a young mother myself, I don't understand how a mother can just stop wanting to be a mother. That's a question I've asked myself all my life.

My mother was too busy worrying about money and material things to be a mom. I only saw her on holidays or during the summertime, when she wasn't breaking her promise to spend time with me. Even then she was only there part of the time.

She was dating this guy, and I fell in love with him. He became my godfather, and he was the best. After they broke up, he was still always there for me. He got married and his wife even took me in as her goddaughter. They were always there, even after they had their own kids. I can say he was one of the men in my life who never let me down and I will always love him for that.

My father wasn't ready to be a parent either. He preferred to chase women than be a full-time father, but he did try to be a part-time dad. He wasn't good at that role either. My father was never really around, but when he was there, he always said to me, "You're dumb. You'll never amount to anything." If a child is told that all her life, she believes it, even if it's not true. She's going to believe it and carry it into her future.

My father met someone and their relationship became serious. He moved in with her and it was OK, but she was really mean. I was only 6 years old at the time, and I didn't like a lot of different types of foods. She insisted I either eat or go to bed, so I told my grandparents. They took me from my dad and I grew up in their house. That mean lady is still in my life, and now I call her my "other" mother. We ended up developing a very close relationship.

On top of all of this, I was molested by a family member. That didn't help my trust in men either. It happened a few times, but my boyfriend took care of that and it never happened again. No one in my family knew except two other people, my sister and a friend. Neither of my parents knew because they weren't there.

That's how my feelings of being unloved and unwanted began. My real mom always sent me the best of everything, including clothes, jewelry and shoes. My dad also made sure I didn't need anything, but they were both wrong. What I needed more than anything was free, and they didn't give it to me. I needed their love.

Years went by, and as a teenager, I was still looking for the love I was missing. I met my oldest son's father around this time. Being 17, he was a lot older than I was at 14 years old. When we started to talk, I was so scared I didn't know what I was doing. We talked for months, then he started to kiss me. That's all we did for a while, then our kisses progressed to touching.

Next, it became, "I love you so much. If you love me, then you will make love to me." Those are the famous words a man will tell you just to get in your pants. I believed him, and we had sex. After that, I had all these different feelings racing though my entire body that I didn't understand. I thought I was in love, so I slept with him again. This time, though, I ended up pregnant.

I was 15 years old, still a kid myself, so I did what a lot of young girls do — I ran away from home. I was missing for five days, and was so scared. I didn't know I was worrying my family out of their minds. My cousin Bug found me and took me back home.

I explained that I ran away because I was pregnant and scared. My grandparents were very hurt. My dad was at the house too, and he was pissed. I really didn't understand why he was upset; he didn't even raise me. He called my mom, who told me I better have an abortion. I told her I wasn't having one and she couldn't make me.

She yelled, "I'm your mother!"

"Since when?" I asked.

That pissed her off. "I'm on my way."

"And?" I challenged.

With all of this going on, neither one of my parents said, "Look, everyone makes mistakes. We'll help you." It was my cousin Bug who did almost everything for my son and me. My grandparents helped, and so did my son's father, Fred. I was blessed he was there for our son.

Fred told me he loved me so much, and that if another man was to say anything to me he would hurt them badly — I mean really badly. If he saw me talking to a man, he hit me. That happened on a regular basis, and the beatings got worse. I became so afraid of him.

Once, he took my son for two weeks and wouldn't tell me where he was. The police wouldn't help me either, so when he came by one time, I started to destroy his car. That's when he finally told me where my son was. I went and got my son, and that was the end of my relationship with Fred.

After we broke up, Fred and I remained friends for our son's sake. We were still in love with each other, and became really close, but I didn't want to fight anymore. I was tired of it all, so we parted ways.

Eventually, I met a new man, Ben. My cousin Donna and I went to a concert in Saginaw, Mich., and Ben was a member of a popular group that was performing. This concert, however, wasn't the first time we met.

Ben and I shared a mutual friend. One day, Ben was out taking a ride because he had just broken up with his girlfriend and was upset. While my friend and I were driving around, we ran into him in Dawn Donuts' parking lot.

My friend introduced us, and Ben asked me to get out and turn around so he could see all of me. After we went back and forth about it for a minute, I finally got out and he said, "Wow, you don't have any backyard. I could never talk to you." He thought he hurt my feelings, but he didn't. By that time in my life, I had built up a wall, so hurting me was very hard to do. I told him to never say never.

We ended up reconnecting at the concert that night, and Ben wanted me bad. I finally gave him my number. The next day he called, and we talked on the phone all night. A week went by and he asked me out on a date. I agreed, and had the best time of my life.

Ben and I spent every day together. We stayed in hotel rooms every day, and he got me whatever I wanted. He started taking me around his friends and family, and not even a week later, he told me he wanted to be with me forever. I believed him, and we ended up having sex. This went on for months and everything was going fine until Ben's supposed best friend told him I was seeing someone else.

That's when Ben started acting crazy as hell. I wasn't seeing anyone, but his best friend didn't know that. He had seen me with Fred, my son's father, and assumed I was cheating on Ben. When Ben found out who I was with, things went downhill.

I already had a man who beat on me really badly before, but I didn't know what Ben would do. I didn't realize his intentions of not letting me go until he made it very clear that if he couldn't have me no one would. Now I had two crazy-ass men in my life. Fred hated Ben and Ben felt the same way, so they always stayed in conflict over me.

Months went by, and Fred went back to an old girlfriend. A year later, Fred was murdered. He was keeping our son when he was shot in the head and face outside the home he was living in with his ex-girlfriend. When I got to the scene and was told that my son was also dead, I fainted right there on the sidewalk. I came to, and was told that my son was OK, that someone had dropped him off at Fred's mother's house.

This was one of the worst days of my life. I lost my first love, the father of my son. He meant the world to me. I was so empty I didn't know what to do. I truly loved that man with everything in me. Thank God I had two best friends, Jean and Noka. They were there for me every day and still are.

Two years after Fred was killed, Ben and I were still dating. Ben was out doing his thing, but had me locked up in our apartment. I couldn't go anywhere unless I was with him or his family, so I wasn't really seeing my family much at all. If I did see them, he took me over and picked me up when I was ready to leave.

We were expecting our first child together, but I ended up having a miscarriage and almost died from it. I was in the hospital while Ben was out with another woman. He wouldn't come and visit me, but when I was released he told me it was my fault our baby died.

Soon after I lost the baby, Ben had to go on the road. He was gone for about four months. When he came home, I cooked like I was told, and the apartment was clean. I knew if things weren't done, there would be hell to pay. Ben mentally abused me, and we even got into it a couple of times, but after I fought back it never happened again.

Don't get me wrong, not all of the relationship was bad. We had a lot of good times too. Ben did really love me, he just didn't know how to show it. He's still not good at it.

After a while, I was pregnant a second time. This time around, Ben was happy and was doing everything a woman could want. Then one day he started a fight with me. Afterward, he went to his mom's, and that's when I learned a woman was staying there with a baby. Come to find out, the kid Ben told me was a godson was actually his child. I realized men lie a lot, and being seven months pregnant, I was really hurt.

Despite his betrayal, Ben and I stayed together. He told me he really loved me and would never do it again. Being in love with him, I believed his lies.

After our son was born, it didn't get any better. We were in a relationship for 13½ years and he continued to cheat. When I couldn't and wouldn't take anymore, I put him out. That's when we really started to fight. It got to a point where he tried to kill me on more than one occasion.

He finally calmed down a little, and we went our separate ways. What no one knew, however, was that we were still sleeping together for years after that, until I ended it. He never wanted to stop, but eventually he realized those days were over and we made it official.

After these relationships, I had a wall up that no man could break down to destroy me. However, I was so good at destroying my own life, the wall I put up to protect myself didn't matter. I was so damn hurt that I started to sleep with men I thought I had feelings for. I was really just looking for love in all the wrong places, and what I was doing was never meaningful.

I continued this cycle until well into my 30s, and it was very hard to stop. During those years, I also started to drink really heavily and made a whole lot of bad decisions, with men and in other areas of my life. I needed to get back in church and pray to the Lord for help.

God put someone in my life when I needed it, and it was my sister Kim. She was the best at helping me get my life in order. She showed me that real love was when someone I loved truly loved me back. My sister Kim was strong, because even though she had her own issues, she was still there for me or anyone else. She helped me get my confidence back.

I enrolled in school to become an EKG technician, PCT technician and phlebotomy technician. When I graduated, Kim and I both worked as phlebotomists for the hospital. I started to feel better about myself, and everything in my life was good.

Then my grandmother who raised me passed away, and I took that really hard. I felt like I was back where I started.

Kim came to the rescue again to help me stay on my feet. She prayed with me every day, no matter what. She talked to me and helped me make the decision to move. Too much was happening to me, and I saw myself starting to do the same stuff again. I moved to Detroit, and she was always there for me. Over the years we became very close, and did everything together, and I mean everything.

Things were going well until Kim was diagnosed with cancer. Like I said, she was strong, and she beat it. My sister went through a lot but never gave up on life or herself. Years passed, and life was good again. We both went back to school, her for nursing and me for cooking. We were so happy.

Then one day, Kim got sick again. I was scared of losing her, and couldn't bring myself to visit until I got a phone call from one of her best friends saying she was dying and only had three days to live. When I received that call, I felt like I was dying as well. I went back to Flint to see my sister and brought my youngest son and cousin Donna with me. Seeing her like that brought us to our knees. Kim lived for those three days, and on the second day I whispered in her ear that I was sorry for not being there, but I knew in my heart she understood.

At the time of the funeral, my son, Donna and I sat with the family. When I saw that our sister listed me as a friend in the obituary, I was upset. That was very hurtful, but nevertheless, I love my sister, even though we still haven't talked since the funeral. I just keep praying that she will forgive me for whatever I did.

In spite of all of the hurt I have been through, I am very happy with myself. I am still single, but content. I finished school at the top of my class with a 3.8 grade point average, something my parents said I would never do. I'm also writing a cookbook on appetizers and drinks.

I have two sons, three grandkids and one daughter-in-law, all of whom I am very proud. I thank God for them and for the love of my family, close friends and my cousin Donna, who is very special to me.

NOTES

I Wish I Woulda Knew Me Back Then

Cherisse Bradley

I Wish I Woulda Knew Me Back Then

Cherisse Bradley is a Flint, Michigan native whose early foundation in music began at the age of 10. Her natural dance ability was cultivated by studying tap, jazz, hip hop and ballet.

While making strides in her dance career, she sang lead with a local band on a tour in Germany for the troops on Army bases. Upon returning to the States, Cherisse eventually moved to New York and began vocal jazz studies at Long Island University Brooklyn Campus.

While in New York, Cherisse returned home annually to Flint as co-founder, producer, and vocalist along with her sisters and father in the family non-profit tap festival and community outreach TAPOLOGY.

Ms. Bradley is also a featured vocalist in sci-fi electro funk techno band Girls like Bass in NYC with Monstah Black and New York's Dubspot electronic music production and DJ school instructor Michele Darling.

In August of 2013, Cherisse took a huge leap of faith by exposing deeply embedded childhood wounds as an incest survivor at the hands of her stepfather in a dream project. She added the role of a sexual assault advocate to her resume and founded I Found My Voice, a creative arts wellness movement for survivors of domestic violence and sexual abuse.

Ms. Bradley currently resides in Flint, Michigan. Her future plans are to expand the I Found My Voice movement, travel, release the Girls Like Bass album and continue development of her solo musical project, which will consist of various musical forms of house, jazz, and soul along with multimedia expression of her obstacles and life triumphs.

SEVENTEEN
Cherisse Bradley

I was 17 years old, and one of my closest friends had just gotten accepted into Eastern Michigan University and she wanted to celebrate. "Celebration" meant a dime bag of weed while riding around laughing and listening to music, and I was always down for that. But this time we added something a little extra … a 40 ounce of Old English 800 apiece. This was a deadly combination to say the least, because it was the first time I had ever drank a whole 40 ounce of beer and I was pretty drunk.

We smoked the weed and drank the beer and proceeded to ride around town for a little while. It didn't take long for her sexual desires to creep up, and of course she wanted to dump me off somewhere. I was a virgin, which seemed somewhat out of style to her and a lot of kids our age. She wasn't, and would tease me about it all the time. The teasing would bother me sometimes, but not for the reasons you think.

It would bother me because she had no idea what I had experienced as a child. I had been sexually abused by my stepfather for five years. He performed oral sex on me until it brought me to orgasm constantly, and taught me how to perform it on him. I had never been penetrated vaginally by his penis, so in that respect I was still a virgin. However, the orgasms had become a lifestyle and were something I could not talk

19

about with my friends. While they were playing on swings and monkey bars, I was already seasoned and knew what an orgasm felt like, so I remained silent.

I stuffed all those experiences and emotions deep inside and continued to grow up the best way I knew how. At that age, I knew a couple of things for sure. I was talented — I could sing, dance and act, and I wanted my first sexual experience of penetration to be something special. I wanted it to be different than what was imposed on me as a child. Those were things I felt I had "control" over.

My grades and focus in school were very poor by this time. Skipping school to smoke weed and hang out was my favorite pastime besides the dance studio or the theater. The creative arts were the only areas where I worked really hard, because they were the only things that made me feel like I was special.

Well, there was one more thing that made me feel special, my boyfriend at the time.

When my girlfriend asked me where I wanted to be dropped off, I told her his house. We pulled up in the driveway and he was sitting on the porch. I had on a pink knit dress that hugged my slim, toned figure, white flats, dark sunglasses and my wet *n* wild pink lipstick to match. I will never forget it.

She hung around with us for a bit in the front yard while we blasted music from the car and danced and laughed. He sat on the porch, watching. This went on for about 20 minutes until she left. He stood up, walked toward me, grabbed my hand and led me into the house and downstairs to his bedroom in the basement. This was not out of the ordinary because I had been down there many times with him. We would always kiss, along with heavy petting, but for some reason this time I felt scared.

We walked in his bedroom and I just stood there feeling like a stiff, frozen brick while my belly was trembling. He put his hands on my shoulders and slipped off the knit dress, which quickly fell to the floor. I remember saying, "I don't want to do it," but he just continued as if I had said nothing. He coaxed me onto the bed, touching me, leaning me backward, and taking off my panties and bra.

I was terrified and didn't want to do it. I tried to get up, but I was so drunk and it was really difficult to try and move from underneath him. I was very reluctant, but he didn't care. I tried to keep my legs tightly closed and he pried them apart with his knee, flinging them back open. He had never been in between my legs without my underwear on, so this was a very scary feeling. I did not want to do it. I kept mumbling, "No," and tried to scoot off the bed. He grabbed my legs and slid me back down.

Then he tried to penetrate me — it was painful. I scooted up and he pulled me back down, each time trying to push a little deeper inside. I didn't want to do it. There were times he would take breaks and start again. I didn't want to do it.

He finally said, "Cherisse, I'm inside you."

I replied, "You are?" I really couldn't tell the difference; all I felt was pressure and pain.

He began to stroke, and all of a sudden I felt a rush of pleasure. I gasped and grabbed him around his neck tightly. Suddenly, he pulled out quickly and rolled over next to me on the bed.

As he pulled out his penis, it was almost like I felt the last bit of myself rush out of me at the same time. I laid there with my legs open and an over-whelming feeling of sadness penetrated deep in my chest. I covered my face with my hands and began to cry. It was the only thing I had left; the only thing I could say was innocent after what my stepfather had done to me as a child. I needed to hold on to that. I wanted it to be special. I longed to love the person whom I would let enter me and for him to love me. This was not the way it was supposed to be.

I remember trying to find my clothes so I could get up and go to the bathroom. I put them on and walked up the stairs. When I reached the top of the stairs, his family was home by then, and everyone just looked at me. It felt as though they could see through my body. I felt like an empty shell. I could not really see their facial expressions, because my vision was so blurry from being drunk, but I knew they were looking at me. I went in the bathroom, wiped myself and saw the blood. I cried all over again.

The next thing I remember is one of his friends driving me home. I think we even had to pull over once so I could throw up.

He called the next day and I was angry, but it didn't last long — we had sex again. I continued to have sex with him because I thought that was how it was supposed to be. Plus, I began to feel the pleasure of being penetrated.

When I told my girlfriends, I was praised and rewarded for finally having become like them. Living under the illusion that losing my virginity was a source of pride, I could now contribute to the conversations with my other sexually active girlfriends. It didn't really register to me that I had been violated, probably because violation was something I was accustomed to. The uncomfortable had become comfortable.

As a young girl I missed so much of the organic wonder, innocence, respect and proper development. I had no clue of the value it brings to the essence of womanhood. As an adult, the responsible world does not care about the abuse I endured that fractured my mental and spiritual capacity. The world just wants "results." In the real world, you have to show up for life and get the job done. This is a hard thing to do when you are not a whole person, when you have been wounded.

Looking back at that experience, I would have done things so differently. The sexual abuse changed the course of my entire life, and I ended up having to do the work of healing as an adult. If only I could go back with what I know now and talk to my 17-year-old self. When my family wanted me to get into therapy for being sexually abused I would have done it. I would have committed to the work of healing myself, learning how to love and forgive and developing my spiritual condition. Surely, I did not deserve the hell I put myself through growing into a young adult with alcohol, sex, and drugs. I had to learn how to forgive myself for the choices I made because I really didn't know any better.

Somewhere along the way I was blessed with the courage to fight for my life. This fight will be a life-long journey, but I have learned, and continue to learn, how to trust and depend on God. I am still mastering how to give myself the love I seek from others. I am responsible for picking up my own pieces. While this is a very painful and harsh reality to face, it's the only way to freedom.

Today, I reflect on the things I have overcome and experience so much gratitude. I am alive. I am healthy and still able to create the life I want for myself. When I have my moments of self-pity, these are the things I hold on to because it didn't have to be this way. There are many women who share my story and did not make it out of their self-made prisons after being abused. They are now dead. I, however, am alive to tell my story and inspire others through art.

Young lady, as you grow and develop, cherish, love, value, protect and challenge yourself. Know your worth. If you are a young, African American girl, educate yourself on our culture. Learn and know black history until it is embedded in your spirit and recognize that you are beautiful no matter what shade you are. If you have been abused, begin the process of healing, even if you think you don't need it and you don't understand it. Learn to trust the process, and to trust God until the day you die. Later in life, the things that will bring you the most grief are not the things you did, but the things you didn't do to enhance your life.

NOTES

Velencia Dixon

Ms. Velencia Dixon is formerly from Flint, Michigan, and currently resides in Charlotte, N.C. She works as a Business Support Manager at PNC Financial Services and owns Word of Mouth Catering, LLC.

Ms. Dixon has over 15 years of professional experience in varying levels of Administrative Support. Previous professional experience includes employment with Bank of America, Wells Fargo and Booz Allen Hamilton.

Velencia holds a Bachelor of Science in Business Management and Master of Science in Management and Leadership from Montreat College. She has two children, Kiairra 19, and Jaylen 16, and in her spare time enjoys reading, shopping and exercising.

TRYING TO FIT IN
Velencia Dixon

The majority of times in my life when I got in trouble at home, church, school or work, or experienced heartache or pain, it was a direct result of me "trying to fit in." As the youngest of three children, I grew up in a middle class home (my parents divorced when I was 10) with no worries. Even though I wasn't shy and had an outgoing personality, I still found it hard to fit in in social environments. As a result of my fear of not fitting in, I made countless bad choices and decisions. After years of soul searching and finding myself, I realized that I was not born to fit in, I was born to stand out!

When I was 14, I had a girlfriend named Tamika. Tamika's father passed away when she was 8 and she was raised by her gay mother and her lover. At Tamika's house, there were few rules. We could stay up as late as we wanted, talk on the phone until all hours of the night and even have guys over. Tamika's mom and lover worked 1st shift, which meant they were gone from the house from six in the morning until four in the afternoon. Based on her mom's work schedule, Tamika and her siblings would often skip school and host ditch parties.

Even though Tamika was my best friend and had an extremely wild side, I was focused on school. I never missed a class and always turned in all my homework assignments.

29

One day, Tamika talked me into skipping school to hang at her house at a skip party. Initially I was quite hesitant about going. I was scared as hell. What if the school called my house? What if my parents found out? I had a million questions, and Tamika had a million answers. We came up with a plan for me to leave the house as if I was going to school, but instead of walking to the bus stop, I'd walk to her house. That's exactly what I did.

When I arrived at Tamika's house, there were eight other kids there as well. They had beer, pills and weed. I'd had a sip of beer before and knew it tasted terrible so I wouldn't drink it. I associated pills with being sick and I didn't know who the pills belonged to or exactly what kind of pills they were, so I wouldn't try those either. But I was intrigued by the marijuana.

There were several older kids at the party who were friends of Tamika's older brother. One of the guys rolled five joints. He lit them up and passed them around. As I smoked the weed, I began to have all the side effects associated with marijuana use. I was paranoid, had the giggles, followed by the munchies.

Tamika's brother Justin put on some music, and we all started dancing. The party was hyped. More kids came, and before you knew it, there were 50 kids in a three-bedroom house. In the midst of the party, Justin cornered me, kissed me and felt on my breast. He told me he had liked me for a very long time. I was flattered. I had a crush on Justin too. He was 17, I was 14 and I'd always secretly fantasized about him kissing me. Before I realized it, we were in his room kissing and making out. There was another couple in the room on the opposite bed doing the same thing. I was very nervous and totally scared, but to fit in, I kept my mouth shut. Justin kissed my neck, then my breast. It felt so good, that when he started unbuttoning my pants, I didn't stop him.

Since I was only 14, I didn't realize what was happening until it was over. Justin had broken my virginity. I went to the restroom and saw the blood and was horrified. My vagina hurt terribly and I still was in disbelief that I'd just had sex for the first time with my best friend's brother and we'd done it in the same room with another couple. I was embarrassed and disgusted with myself. I sat in Tamika's room out of shame until it was time for me to go home.

I went home as if I'd gone to school, but I was in pain. I was too embarrassed and ashamed to tell anyone about my experience. This was one of the first times in my life I made a bad decision to fit in, but it wouldn't be the last.

August 18, 1992, I entered college as a freshman at Eastern Michigan University. I'd never lived away from my parents and their watchful eyes. The feeling of independence I felt was overwhelming. I was used to my mother telling me to do my chores and giving me a curfew.

In college, I did as I wanted, when I wanted, with little to no repercussions. I had a roommate and suitemates. The girls and I got along well. Our rooms were the party rooms. I stayed in a coed dorm, so the people next to us were guys. They were really cool also and partied a lot too.

One day, my neighbors decided to have an informal party in their room. My roommate and I were invited, so we decided to start our party before we went to the neighbors' room. Even though none of us were of the legal drinking limit, we bought a bottle of vodka and proceeded to make "screwdrivers," or vodka and orange juice. We were drunk before we arrived at the party.

When we arrived, our neighbors greeted us at the door with more drinks and a few hits of acid. I'd had plenty of alcohol before, but never used or even tried acid. I, along with my roommates, took the drinks and acid our hosts had graciously provided. I was scared to try the acid, but my roommates weren't. I didn't want to seem like a square, so to fit in, I did a half of a hit of acid. The feeling I had from the acid is indescribable. I prayed to God that I would come down from the high and vowed I would never try hard-core drugs again.

The day after the party, my neighbors were expelled from school. Apparently, one of the girls left the party and was in an automobile accident. Since the girl was underage, the police demanded to know where she'd obtained the liquor. She quickly told on my neighbors; thus they were expelled. I thank God that I didn't get caught up in that mess. Unfortunately, that didn't stop me from trying to fit in in social settings.

The last encounter I had trying to fit in occurred when I was 24 years old. I'd recently moved to the South and was trying to get acclimated to the new environment. I noticed that several of the young women I encountered when I was at the various night clubs were always getting into fist fights. It was "fashionable" to fight in North Carolina, or so I thought. I thought if I got into a fight I'd fit in more socially.

One night after partying until the early hours of the morning, I returned to my friend's house to retrieve my vehicle. While I was leaving the complex, I had an altercation with a resident. The resident hit my car with her hand. I felt very disrespected, so I got out and started hitting the girl. Her friends jumped in the fight, as did mine. It was early March, so it was still cold outside and there was also a little snow on the ground. As we fought, we fell in the snow and dirt.

After fighting for what seemed like an eternity, someone in the crowd of onlookers broke up the fight. The only injury I suffered was a scratch on my face. I went home and dusted myself off, and that was the end of it.

My dad saw me the day after the fight and asked about the scratch on my face. I explained what happened, but did not want a lecture from my dad about fighting, so I didn't tell him I was drunk when the fight started.

I listened intently to the message my father was trying to convey. The message was that fighting is never worth it. The fight could've been worse. I could've been seriously injured or I could've seriously injured someone else. Someone could've taken my life over something meaningless. I was super pissed with myself after the conversation with my father. He made me realize that trying to "fit in" is not worth it. Fitting in does not make you memorable, but standing out does.

NOTES

I Wish I Woulda Knew Me Back Then

Pya Harris-Flanagan

Pya Harris-Flanagan was born and raised in Flint, Michigan. She is a divorced mom of three lovely daughters. Pya is the daughter of Carla Harris and Albert Williams, and was co-raised by the late Mr. and Mrs. Clinton and E. Ann Harris. She is one of six siblings from these families.

Ms. Flanagan attended Flint Public Schools, graduating from Flint Northwestern High School. She attended Mott Community College as a Criminal Justice major, later changing her major to Respiratory Therapy. She is currently employed with the General Motors Corporation, where she serves as an EMR.

Ms. Flanagan is an active member of Local 659, where she currently serves as a Joint Counsel recording secretary. She is a lifelong member of the New Jerusalem Full Gospel Baptist Church, as well as a former member of Victorious Christian Women.

Pya is an active community volunteer with many organizations. She gets great joy from attending and participating in her daughters' many activities, such as Girls Scouts, cheerleading, basketball and modeling.

FOLLOW YOUR ROAD MAP, BE WHO YOU ARE
Pya Harris-Flanagan

I wish I knew me back then, the real me, not the person everyone said I was. I wish I knew the person who knew where she was going and how to get there. I wish I would have known how to follow my dream, my own road map, and not other people's dream or plan for me. I would have followed the life plan that, with the help of God, of course, was chosen just for me. I would be so much further ahead in life.

Instead, I followed the life plan that others said I should follow, only to find out later in life that was never my plan or the plan God had for me. Wow, how could I have been so blind? Only one word can explain it, love — not the love I had for myself, but the love I had for others.

Yes, I know God teaches us that He is love and to love other people. But you have to first learn to love yourself and know that you matter. So you have to first love God, then yourself, and He will give the order in how you should love everyone else, because after all, if you are not operating in the place where you should be, chances are you will not be happy.

And if you're not happy, how can you be a positive person, or even bring a positive attitude to situations in your life? That's how you usually end up on another road operating in someone else's dream or life plan. You end up totally off of the course in the life you started or that you should be on. In other words, you are lost.

I can still hear it so loud and clear as if it was yesterday. "You're not ready to be married. You are too smart to be married right now. You need to finish school and get your degree and become a lawyer first." Boy, oh boy how I wish I had listened.

You see, I was 19 years old and thought I knew it all. After all, I had a job, my own car, and a child I was raising (even though she was not biologically mine, I loved her with all my heart). I even had an apartment I shared with my sisterly-cousin, as I liked to call her. How many people were doing all these things at my age? Not many. I had everything that I thought a "grown" or "adult" person was supposed to have and I was very content.

Between the ages of 20 and 21, it seemed as if I had the "Midas touch." Everything was going my way. I seemed to be on top of the world, and all my dreams were headed in the right direction. I had a good family that loved me and I loved them even more, a great job with benefits, 401k, an unlimited earning potential, a brand new car, and two different men bouncing in and out of my life. This was where I started to get off my road map.

Everything was going great and I was happy. Then it happened. I fell in love with one of the men I was dating, and decided to start bringing him around my family. That was when things got out of hand.

The famous question my relatives always asked every couple who announced they were together was, "So, when are you all getting married?" What? Up until that point I had never thought about marriage. I mean, I was always a bridesmaid; that was my part. I was supposed to be a bridesmaid in my sisterly-cousin's wedding, and maid of honor in my cousin Fantasy's wedding, but that was it.

Being married was the furthest thing from my mind, even though my family always had a strong belief in marriage. But it was around that time my mind completely shifted. Everyone else was getting married and I wasn't. I feared the judgment and ridicule. After all, I was raised in the church and I convinced myself it was better to marry than to burn.

My life would never be the same after my family asked us that question.

From the minute we got to the car, my happy mood disappeared, and I said, "Why aren't we getting married?" in an aggravated tone. "Everyone else is getting married, why aren't we?"

I remembering him saying, "You're not ready to be married. You have a great job. Let's wait until you finish school and I get a better job before we get married."

After that day, our lovely relationship became a living nightmare, one argument after another. Finally, he left town for a better job and I'm sure he wanted to get away from me as well.

Soon after that, I started to become close to the other man again. He was very different than the man I was dating before. He was easy to talk to and always knew just what to say. Plus, he wanted to get married and was instantly ready to walk down the aisle.

It became official — we were a couple. Two months later we were engaged. Things were moving so fast. I wasn't going to school, was barely going to work, and not even seeing my family. All I was doing was concentrating on getting married like everyone else. My life was going in a whole different direction. I'd left church and all the choirs I had grown up singing with. My fiancé said the church people were "all in our business," whatever that meant.

Then, one morning I woke up "sick," so I went to the doctor, and sure enough, I was pregnant. Now I had two problems. One, everyone in my family disliked this man, and two, I still was not married. I was raised partially by my aunt and uncle, who were very religious and had stern morals about having children and not being married. My natural mother was more laidback about marriage, but even she was not going to be happy with this situation. Oh boy, what am I going to do? I thought.

I just kept going right on with my life and didn't say anything, but a sudden trip to the hospital changed all of that. I miscarried my child, and for the first time in over a year I spoke to God. It was one of the darkest points in my life. The next night, I returned to work; after all, I was the only one working. Two weeks later, I went to see the doctor, who was a close family friend. I found out I was still pregnant. What a blessing! I was so grateful. The Lord had not forgotten me even when I had forgotten Him.

After the birth of my first child, I was so grateful for her and so ashamed at the same time. I stayed as far away from my family and the church as possible. A few months later, my dream came true — we were married. Things began to move even faster than before. I was way off my road map now. I had no idea of the dangers that lay ahead. My life was spinning completely out of control. I was working more and more and my husband was coming home less and less often, and when he did, he always made sure I regretted his presence.

After finding out I was pregnant with my third child, I knew I had to get back on my road. I had nothing — no car, no house, and was barely holding on to my job. Where did I go wrong? Whose life plan was this? This was not the life I had planned. Was wanting to be married like everyone else worth this? Why didn't I stick to the road I was on? I was lost and I had to find my way back to the right road, the road that was designed for Pya and no one else.

How do you find out if you are on the right road? It's simple. Are you happy on the road that you are on? Is this life fulfilling to you? If not, why? It's time to make the necessary adjustments.

First, figure out how you got on this road. Is it your plan or the plan of someone else? Make the adjustments to get off, even if it means changing your friends or even separating from some family members (because you can't pick family members). They may be angry, but remember, if they truly love you, they will understand.

Second, I always pray for strength, and in some cases I do this first. Think about how you got to the place or predicament you are in, and evaluate what you are going to have to do to change it.

Third, after you figure it out, take the necessary actions. It may look impossible or even scary. Find positive quotes and repeat them to yourself. For example, I always use "I can do all things through Christ that strengthens me." Find another positive quote, but remember, it needs to work for you. Also, know that you are usually a lot stronger than you give yourself credit for. You've been riding on a long, far road for however long, but guess what? You're still in the driver's seat. It's time to be who you are, operate in the real you and follow the road plan of your life!

Be blessed!

NOTES

I Wish I Woulda Knew Me Back Then

Turjemia Flowers

Turjemia is a dedicated spoken word artist, novelist, and blogger. She was born and raised in Arkansas. She wrote her first novel, *Betraying Ayanna*, which was inspired by real life experiences. Her book is available everywhere online, including Amazon, Barnes & Noble, Books-a-Million, etc.

Ms. Flowers is also a dedicated advocate to bringing awareness toward child abuse, as well as domestic violence. Aside from writing, she enjoys traveling, creating music, and shopping.

Visit Turjemia's website for the latest updates: www.turjemia.com.

HE DIDN'T DESERVE MY SACREDNESS
Turjemia Flowers

One day, my mom sent me to the store with a grocery list. I was shopping alone when some random guy appeared out of nowhere. He approached me with a flirty glare. I was unsure of what to say because his swagger was thuggish, yet I felt honored that someone of his caliber found me attractive. I compared him to most of the boys at school, and he was totally different. He examined my body from head to toe and licked his lips before he opened his mouth to speak. I loved the attention I received. It caused me to feel confident about myself. His skin was caramel, his eyes were light brown, and his hair was dark and curly. His cologne smelled delicious.

"What's up, lil mama?" he asked.

"Nothing, just doing a little shopping."

"You look so sexy." His voice was sensual. I was about to melt.

"I'm Jason, and I want to get to know you better."

"Really?" I asked.

"You are the best looking woman I've ever seen."

"Thanks, but I'm still in high school," I explained.

"How old are you?"

49

"Sixteen."

We exchanged numbers, and I was on top of the world. For the first time, I felt just like a super model. I turned to walk away, and his eyes were stuck to my butt.

"Stay by the phone when you get home," he said, winking.

Later that night, the phone rang. I was excited to see his number on the Caller ID. I picked up, and my heart was racing. It was ready to burst out of my blouse. My palms were sweaty; I was nervous. We talked on the phone for most of the night. I was hoping I wouldn't get caught on the phone since I was sneaking behind my mother's back.

I was infatuated with the idea of having a boyfriend, but the household rules were strict, and I wasn't allowed to date. I wanted to transform myself because I didn't feel special. I wanted to look beautiful, like most of the girls in school, but my mother wouldn't let me dress in the latest styles. I wanted to wear makeup, and get my hair done at the salon. I couldn't do any of those things because my mother was old-fashioned. I wasn't allowed to express myself, so I kept all of my true feelings bottled up inside.

My self-esteem was low. I was considered the underdog at school, and wasn't popular at all. My mother didn't understand me, so I pretended to be a perfect kid. She wasn't the easiest person to talk to, so most of the time, I chose to handle things on my own.

Things progressed quickly, and Jason and I were dating after a few phone conversations. He was sweet-natured, and listened to me whenever I was upset with my mom. He helped me feel comfortable, and knew how to make me feel important. Unlike my mom, Jason never yelled at me, nor did he call me out of my name. I was afraid my mom would become suspicious of my secret relationship with him.

Jason was the first guy I ever kissed. He grabbed my hand, and nibbled the tip of each finger. It was the most romantic thing that a guy had ever done to me. Since he was my first boyfriend, I became curious about sex and couldn't stop fantasizing about it. Jason and I talked about sex a lot. Many of my friends had already lost their virginity by the time they were 11 years old, so I'd heard many stories about it from them.

I snuck out of the house to be with Jason on several occasions. He would wait for me around the corner, and I'd hop into the car with him. One time, we drove around for a little while, and he took me to a nearby park. There were no other cars in the parking lot. He began to nibble on my ears, and I couldn't resist his charm.

"Are you going to let me be the first man to make love to you?" he asked flirtatiously.

"I'm a little nervous," I said.

"Don't worry, I'll be gentle."

"I'm not really sure if I want to do this."

"Baby, I promise I'm going to make you feel good, all you have to do is relax."

When I gave my virginity to Jason, I was terrified. It was too late to change my decision because I already promised him that I would have sex that night. I didn't want him to lose interest in me. He took his time by kissing me all over, but I wasn't sure of what to expect next. It lasted for a few minutes, and surprisingly, it wasn't as good as everyone had said it would be. As a matter of fact, it only caused me to feel icky, and somewhat disgusted with myself. Afterward, I realized I was no longer considered pure in God's eyes. I went home to take a shower, then laid in my bed. Later, I reminisced about my first sexual experience, and suddenly my feelings toward Jason were beginning to grow stronger.

The following week, I wanted to surprise him, so I went to visit him at his mother's house. I walked to the front door and rang the doorbell. A girl approached, about seven months pregnant. She came to the door with an ugly attitude. She put her hands on her hips and stared at me as if I had done something wrong. I didn't know who she was. I'd never seen her a day in my life.

"Is Jason home?" I asked.

"No he's not, and who wants to know?"

"His girlfriend," I responded.

"Are you kidding me?" she snapped.

I stood speechless, and didn't know what else to say. My tongue was dry, and I couldn't open my mouth.

"I'm seven months pregnant with his baby!"

"Well, he didn't tell me he was seeing someone," I explained.

"Jason and I have been dating for two years, and we're planning to get married next month."

I was tongue-tied, and suddenly my heart weighed about a thousand tons. Shocked, I wanted to cry, but I managed to hold back my tears. I did not want to give his baby mama the pleasure of seeing the painful depth of my real emotions. My body felt cold and my feet were frozen, as heavy as blocks of ice.

Out of nowhere, Jason appeared, and he looked nervous to see me and his baby mama conversing. He grabbed the pregnant girl by the hand. "Come on, baby, let's go."

He ignored me as if I wasn't standing there. I wanted to slap him for being a jackass. Not only did he lie about his age, but he also lied about having a pregnant girlfriend. Turns out, he was actually 22 years old, and the entire time I thought he was only 18. I decided to walk away because I knew this would be the end of our relationship. At that moment, I realized I gave my precious virginity to a liar who didn't deserve it.

My mother and I still couldn't get along. Our relationship was weak, and there was hardly any communication between the two of us. She cursed me out until I'd almost forgotten my real name. The verbal abuse caused me to become rebellious toward her. She yelled each time she mentioned my name. I hated to hear the sound of her voice at times. She tried to embarrass me whenever my friends were around and never understood how bad the humiliation was. She pushed me into a deep depression, and I felt the need to talk it over with her. I tried to open up about my feelings, but it was difficult because she didn't understand any of my emotional pain. She would tell me to stop whining like a baby.

As a result, I was forced to accept things for what they really were. Most of the time, I suffered silently inside my room. I was trapped inside of a shell, and I wasn't allowed to exert my self-expression. The household was an emotional prison, and she was the security guard who kept my happiness locked away from me. She treated me as if I was the enemy, instead of her daughter.

The next month, my period was late, and I became scared. I thought I was pregnant. I was also afraid to tell my mother I was no longer a virgin. I decided to keep my secret to myself, but the agony was tough to endure. I couldn't breathe because there were so many hidden emotions inside of me.

There were times when Jason and I would accidentally cross paths with one another whenever I was out in public. I couldn't force myself to look at him, because I was still hurt by how things went down. The way he treated me and how he lied to me were the ultimate heartbreak. I put so much of my trust in him, and he pretended to love me. He made me feel special in the beginning, but as soon as I gave him my virginity, he changed his ways. He became distant, and didn't return any of my calls anymore.

It was hard for me to let go since I was still emotionally attached to him. I felt like a fool for believing everything he promised me. I was supposed to be his wife, but there was another woman in his life. I felt jealous of her because I should've been the lady on his arm. He was already in the process of starting a new life with someone else and there wasn't enough room for me.

Once I found out the truth, he gave me the boot. He treated me as if I was another notch on his belt buckle. Since we already had sex, I was no longer of any value to him. He didn't consider me as special as he said. I had become just like the other girls at school. I couldn't believe how fake he was, and it wasn't fair!

My relationship with my mom was skating on thin ice. I started doing drugs to get my mind off the problems that were going on at home. I began to smoke weed with the rest of my friends whenever I hung on the block. Whenever I decided to get high with them, it was an escape from my painful reality. They showed me love and helped me feel important.

One day, my mother was doing some laundry, and a blunt fell out of the pocket of my jeans. She brought it to my attention because she was extremely upset about it.

"Why are you bringing drugs into my house?" she screamed.

"It's not mine," I lied.

"If it isn't yours, then who does it belong to?"

"A close friend asked me to keep it, and I forgot to give it back."

"Are you lying to me?" she hissed.

"No, I swear I'm telling the truth," I bargained.

"Okay, we'll see about that." She took the blunt and put it away, then picked up the phone to make a call. There was attitude in her body language.

I stood back and bit my lip because I knew I was lying but didn't want to get in trouble. The blunt was mine but I couldn't tell her the truth. I was nervous because I didn't know whose number she was dialing.

Thirty minutes later, the police arrived. I was shocked that she decided to sell me out to the cops! The officer approached me, and placed handcuffs on my wrists. The grip was tight, and very uncomfortable. He looked at me and announced, "You're coming with me, young lady."

My tears were trapped inside the walls of my eyes. I couldn't believe my mother! I looked back at her. "How could you do this to me?"

"No child of mine will be bringing drugs into my house and lie about it!" she yelled.

The police escorted me to sit in the back of the police car, and my mother stood there with her arms folded. The expression on her face was filled with anger. She didn't have any sympathy toward me, and I was disappointed with her decision to call the police. They treated me as if I was a criminal. It was degrading and very embarrassing. All of the neighbors watched as they took me away. I placed my face into my hands; the humiliation was too much for me to bear. Some of my classmates were pointing and laughing at me as I rode in the backseat of the police car.

Because of the charge, the police gave me a drug test. After I tested positive for marijuana, they sent me to rehab. I stayed there for three months and became extremely homesick because I wanted to get out of that place. I grew tired of seeing the hospital staff each day. The food was horrible, and I missed my bed from home. The mattresses at rehab were thin. I could feel the springs poking my back each night.

They gave me a pregnancy test, and I was thankful when the results were negative. It was a sigh of relief, but my happiness had gone down the drain. I was lost and confused at the same time.

My mother didn't come to visit me, and I often felt lonely. I noticed the other teenagers' families would come to see them each week. I became sad because my family wasn't around to support me. I had no one to talk to, and it was miserable. I decided to write a letter to my mother.

Dear Mom,

I'm sorry I lied to you. Sometimes I want to talk, but you always seem to yell at me whenever I want to express myself to you. I don't know how to talk about anything because you don't treat me as if I'm your daughter. There are times when you make me feel as if I'm a stranger. I know you're not happy with my decision to smoke weed, but it's the only way I can release the pain. I hope you don't become angry when you decide to read this letter. I want to have a closer relationship with you. I would like to go shopping and do fun things, just like most mothers and daughters. I hope you will find it in your heart to forgive me for the mistakes I've made.

Love,

Your Daughter

I sent the letter, but she never wrote back. I couldn't help but ponder over the way she didn't respond to me. Does she hate me or something? What could it be?

Weeks later, I was released from rehab, and my mom was standing there. She waited for me to come to the exit door with my belongings. I was so happy that she had come to take me home. She grabbed me, and squeezed me with a tight hug.

"I read your letter, and it brought tears to my eyes."

I felt grateful she said something about the letter. It was a very sentimental moment, and it showed me that she actually cared.

We hopped into the car, and she drove me home. As soon as we entered the house, I could smell the aroma of a German Chocolate cake. I grew excited because it had been three months since I had some cake. When I was in rehab, we didn't have any desserts. My taste buds watered for some sugary sweets.

"Did you bake this for me?" I asked.

"Yes, it's all yours, so enjoy." She sat a full glass of milk in front of me.

"Thanks," I said in between bites, and washed it down with milk.

After I finished eating the cake, I assisted her with the dishes.

"Thanks for helping me out," she said.

I smiled at her, and she smiled back! She wasn't yelling or cursing, and there was a sense of peace in the room. For some reason, I felt there was a change in our relationship. Even though she didn't respond to my letter, it was obvious it had touched her after she read it. I went to the mall one day, and Jason appeared out of nowhere. He walked up to me, and I tried to play tough by ignoring him. He stopped me and gently grabbed me by the arm. "Hey, where are you going?"

I quickly snatched my arm away from him with an attitude.

"Why are you grabbing on me?"

"Just wanted to tell you I'm sorry for the way I treated you."

"It's too late to apologize," I snapped.

"Look, I know you're still upset with me, but I was hoping we could work this out."

"You're so full of it. I refuse to listen to this crap." I turned to walk away, and he pulled me back a second time.

"Baby, please don't go, I need you," he begged.

Once again, my feelings were beginning to take control of my decision to give him a second chance. I wanted Jason to love me because I loved him. I tried to ignore the fact that he was expecting a baby with another woman, but the thought wouldn't leave my mind. I couldn't stomach being the chick on the side; I wanted to be the only girl in his world.

"I can't let you hurt me again."

He kissed my cheek, and softly tilted my chin, forcing me to stare deeply into his gorgeous eyes. I was beginning to feel weak for his charm, but I knew he was still a loser.

"I promise I'll be there for you, baby," he said gently.

"But you're engaged to someone else."

He chuckled. "I'm not engaged. She's lying!"

"I don't believe you, because you're a liar."

I walked away, feeling proud of myself, but it wasn't an easy decision. I couldn't stop the tears from pouring down my cheeks.

I made it home, and mom was cooking. Her apron was wrapped around her waist, and the scent of gravy pork chops and mashed potatoes danced in the air.

"Are you hungry?" she asked.

"No, thanks."

"Is everything alright?"

"Yeah, I'm fine, just a little tired."

I ran into my room to get some privacy, and I cried into my pillow until it was soggy and wet. I didn't want my mother to know that I was upset over a boy. She seemed to be in a good mood, and I didn't want to bother her with my problems. I tried to hide my emotions from her because our relationship was beginning to grow strong. I hadn't smoked any weed since I was released, and things were going well between us. I didn't want to mess it up — it was a dream come true. My mother was no longer being mean toward me, and that was all I could ask for.

She warned me about boys several times, but I decided to have sex anyway. I couldn't build the courage to reveal my secret to her. It felt good that she accepted me as her daughter but I didn't want to disappoint her. I had to prove myself worthy by doing all the right things to keep her happy. I didn't want to give her any reason to call the police again. I wanted to continue to be on good behavior to keep a smile on her face.

Meanwhile, I skipped dinner because I was too upset to eat. Mom came into my room to check on me. I was bundled underneath my covers, and didn't want to be bothered because I was depressed.

"I put your plate to the side, sweetie," she said.

"I'll eat it later, thanks."

"Are you feeling any better?"

"Not really."

She placed her hand on my forehead. "Are you running a temperature?"

"I'm depressed," I admitted.

She became concerned. I sat up in bed, and when I couldn't hold back any longer, I blurted, "Mama, I think there's something you should know."

She gave me her full attention. I became intimidated by her presence, but I swallowed hard to give myself the courage to spill the beans to her.

"I'm not a virgin anymore."

There was silence in the room while I waited for her to give a response.

"Chile, I already knew."

I became curious. "How did you know?"

"I found some condoms in your room when you were away at rehab," she explained.

A sense of relief fell over me.

"So you're not mad at me?" I asked.

"Well, I wished you would've waited until you were married. It's the right way of doing things," she said.

"I thought I was in love, but he turned out to be a jerk."

"Take it as a lesson learned. You should be thankful you're not pregnant. He probably would've been a deadbeat father to his child. From now on, just keep your legs closed, and you won't have to worry about suffering from any consequences."

I knew my mother was right, so we hugged. I felt relieved that she was being understanding toward my feelings.

I learned a valuable lesson from my mistake. If I could turn back the hands of time, I would've never slept with a man at the age of 16. I would've waited until I was old enough to be married to a husband of my own. I wasn't old enough to have sex, but I decided to grow up before my time by giving my virginity to an older man who was a liar. I was anxious to lose my virginity because I didn't know how to love myself. I didn't understand the importance of sex. I was influenced by the attention he gave me, but it wasn't the right thing to do. Sex isn't meant to be a casual act of affection, but was created for the marriage arrangement by our Creator in the heavens.

It's very important to hold on to your sacredness (virginity), because it's meant to be given to your husband. If you love yourself, you'll cherish your body and wait for the right man to come along. No one should try to rush love, because if you do, you'll end up with a broken heart. The emotional scars are the hardest to face because they can't be erased overnight.

As a result of my actions, I'm left with memories that were preventable, if I would've made the right decision. I was 16 years old when I decided to give my virginity to an undeserving person simply because I was under the illusion that he was someone special. It's not wise to follow your heart in most cases.

My Sacredness

My beauty is more than being naked
My body is a temple; it's sacred
My mind is a vivid treasure
My personality is an exquisite pleasure

My smile is sweeter than any treat
Beautiful from my head to my feet
I'm delightful whenever I speak
I'm too powerful to become weak

I deserve to know my self-worth
God placed me on this earth
I have a purpose
A will to fulfill

I deserve to be treated like a queen
To be married is my dream
I'm not a knockoff
Or a drop off

I'm the wifey type
I don't believe the hype
I will not be misused
Or abused

I deserve to receive the best
I will not settle for less

NOTES

Danielle Green

Danielle Green, born and raised in Flint, Michigan, is the mother of three beautiful daughters, Tia, Alyssa and Makala. Danielle graduated from Mott Community College with a General Studies degree. She went on to receive a Bachelor of Science degree from Central Michigan University in Public Administration with a concentration in Community Development. She is presently pursuing a master's degree in the nonprofit sector.

Danielle is the host of a community talk show called Empower, keeping the community informed on issues that affect them. She is also an actor, best-selling author, keynote speaker, philanthropist and entrepreneur.

Ms. Green has starred in several films, most recently, a film titled "Heartbeat," created to bring awareness to domestic violence. Her directorial debut stage play, "Pray for Me," was released in April 2014. Danielle is also the president of TEAM810, a group of dedicated individuals committed to positive change in Flint.

Danielle Green owns Image Publishings, and is responsible for the publication of *Coulda Shoulda Woulda*, which chronicles her life growing up in Flint. Additionally, she is the driving force behind *I Wish I Woulda Knew Me Back Then,* also a product of her publishing company.

Ms. Green is the founding director of a nonprofit organization, Empower. Its mission is to improve youths' lives and opportunities by developing their capabilities. This is achieved by promoting education, character building and other necessary components that will allow them to live up to their full potential.

Danielle has served as the co-director of My Dreams Do Come True (MDDCT) and is currently the Director of Community Impact. MDDCT serves Mid-Michigan by providing deserving young ladies with new and gently used prom dresses to help them make their dreams come true.

Additionally, Danielle is a Community Representative for Genesee County DHS and a Child Advocate for the YWCA.

Ms. Green has received numerous awards for her work, including a community dedication award and a Courageous Woman award. She was honored with a Proclamation from Flint Mayor Dayne Walling in 2013, formally recognizing November 8th as Danielle Green Day.

For more information about Danielle Green, visit www.empoweringouryouth.info or www.imagepublishings.com.

A GIFT AND A CURSE
Danielle Green

What is beauty? Wait a minute, don't answer that yet.

Webster defines beauty as: beau·ty, noun: the quality of being physically attractive.

Growing up on the north side of Flint was pretty typical for an urban community. My mother was the head of the house, mostly because I had a father who would come and go as he pleased. Having an older sister and a younger brother made me the middle child. We weren't what I would consider poor and we definitely weren't rich. Thanks to Michigan's welfare system, we had mostly everything we needed. We ate well, dressed decent and Section 8 made sure we kept a roof over our heads.

We never knew when we woke if our dad had returned or not. Most times I would be happy to see him. If the smell of bacon, eggs and pancakes filled the house, that usually meant it was going to be a good day. It meant he was in a good mood and no one would get hurt. If he had returned and my mother's door was closed, my stomach would hurt all day. Not knowing what to expect caused me to be a nervous wreck. I constantly had to go to the bathroom and I bit my nails until they bled.

But besides all of that, we didn't have it too bad. My mother took a lot of care when it came to keeping us neat and clean. My sister and I always had barrettes and/or ribbons in our hair that matched our outfits. I'm proud to say we were actually the cleanest, best-dressed kids in the neighborhood. My dad cooked us good meals and he made the best grape Kool-Aid in town. There were even times when he read us stories. They may have been Donald Goines books, but bonding time is bonding time. That's where I developed my love of reading, from my dad. Still today, *Black Girl Lost* and *Whore Son* are two of my favorite novels.

My mother was a light brown, petite, slim lady who kept her appearance up as well. She wore a neat afro that always seemed to be freshly picked out. She had the perfect texture and thickness for it. I wanted to wear one so bad, but my hair just wouldn't cooperate. I have so many good memories of her playing her eight-track tapes as we danced and sang to all the latest hits. The Temptations, Spinner and Four Tops — she had all the jams.

My dad's appearance was exotic, kind of like a lighter version of Erik Estrada from CHiPs. He had black, silky, curly locks of hair that appeared to be oily because they were so shiny.

A combination of both parents, my siblings and I were like a flesh-tone rainbow. I was a shade vanilla, my brother was a shade caramel and my sister was a shade chocolate. It was perfect, or so I thought. In the privacy of our own home we never paid much attention to the difference in our complexions. It just wasn't a big deal to us. Outside of the house it was a completely different story. Strangers and family pointed out my sister's and my differences. "Why are you light and why is she dark?" People frequently asked, "Do y'all have the same mother and father?"

I would often get asked the question, "Are you mixed?" For a long time, I was unaware of what that meant. Keep in mind that growing up in Flint, Michigan, in the 70s, a person of mixed race was fairly uncommon or not something we were used to seeing. Because of my fair skin, long, black, silky hair with a slight curl, in my urban community I looked different than the norm. Knowing what I know now, I can understand why people thought that.

Because of my exterior appearance, I was viewed as a beautiful little girl in most people's eyes. Being "beautiful" came with lots of perks, but it had its downside as well. While some thought I should be praised, others thought I should suffer because of my looks.

I was literally punished as a child, by family members who took it upon themselves to "teach me a lesson." My first memory of this was when I was about four years old. I remember going to the mall with one particular relative, my cousins and my sister. As we drove to our destination, I prayed and asked God to please not let anyone give me any compliments. I didn't want anyone looking at me and smiling, saying how cute I was or touching my hair, saying how long and soft it was. I just wanted to be left alone.

It never failed though, as some nice person would single me out and make me the center of attention. "She is beautiful, what's her name?" Or, "Is that Niecy's daughter?" I just wanted to scream, "Please shut up! You're going to get me in trouble!" At that moment, there wasn't any indication by my relative of what was going to occur once we got back to the house, but I knew.

As I stood there and smiled at the nice stranger who somehow only noticed me and looked past all the other kids, I wanted to cry. I wished I had super powers to make myself invisible, but I guess God didn't hear that prayer either.

On the trip home, everyone was told how pretty, great and smart they were. Everyone except for me, of course; I was totally ignored. On occasion, we stopped at McDonald's and everyone was able to get what they wanted. I remember like it was yesterday.

"Four cheeseburger Happy Meals, please."

I wanted to say, "There are five of us," as I counted in my head to make sure. I silently cried as the other kids laughed, knowing who wasn't going to get one, the "beautiful" little girl.

While the other kids sat in front of the TV watching cartoons and enjoying their food, I was made to sit in the corner and face the wall. It got to the point where I was just glad I was allowed to sit in the same room to hear the TV and smell the food, because I wasn't always allowed that luxury.

The older I became, the more I started to figure this "beautiful" thing out. Like I said before, it came with lots of perks. The perks were extravagant and expensive. I was offered houses, cars, designer clothes, shoes and handbags, all-expense-paid trips and I didn't have to do anything but show up. I was treated like a celebrity, locally and nationally.

Whenever I would go out to eat there was no waiting, and reservations were never necessary. When I went to clubs and celebrity parties, it was VIP only. I, nor anyone who was with me, ever had to wait in line, pay to get in or purchase drinks. These perks just came with being me. The guys, whoever they may have been, made sure I enjoyed myself. They didn't know me, they just liked what they saw, as they often reminded me. It didn't matter if I was a nice person or even a good person.

Anytime I traveled to places like Cali, Miami, New York, etc., the red-carpet treatment became something I expected, and I was never disappointed. I've been able to party with some of the greats, such as Michael Jordan, Allen Iverson, Sean "Puffy" Combs, Tupac, Biggie Smalls, LL Cool J and Will Smith, just to name a few. All I had to do was have my face in the place and be seen by the right person.

I was in a crowd of 20,000 at a Jay Z concert once, and was selected to be escorted backstage, given a VIP pass and again, treated like a star. I met this guy, and even though we barely knew each other, he gave me his car keys and told me to meet him at the club after the concert.

Later that night, my friends and I pulled up to valet parking in my new friend's Mercedes. I stepped out looking like a million dollars, sporting a two-piece red suit with a pair of Valentino pumps and the clutch to match. Security walked us past the super long line that was wrapped around the building. The looks we received were unreal. If looks could kill, we would have been dead.

As soon as we entered the club, my friend was right there to meet me. I introduced him to my friends and he said anything we wanted was on the house. We were escorted to a reserved table that had two bottles of champagne waiting. Even though I didn't drink, I appreciated it.

At this time I still had no idea who the guy was. As my new friend and I were trying to spend some time getting to know each other, we were constantly being interrupted by various celebrities, some I recognized, some I didn't. They wanted to shake his hand, say hello or just hold a conversation. As the night went on I found out why — he was the owner of the club. I wasn't surprised; I usually attracted that type, young, rich and successful. He apologized for all the interruptions as he complimented me on my physical appearance.

As usual, I had a wonderful time and was invited to come back anytime I wanted to. All my friends were so excited, but this was what I was used to. I thanked him for being so kind to me and my friends, but for some reason I was becoming extremely irritated. I was used to superficial men who only wanted to be seen with me. I was even used to so-called friends who wanted to hang around me just because they knew it would be beneficial to them. But I was finally at a point in my life where I wanted someone who wanted to get to know me, the inner me. He was a perfect gentleman, but not once did he ask me about my goals or dreams. He just wanted to take me shopping and dress me up to make himself look good.

As I got older and wiser, I realized these experiences had absolutely nothing to do with who I was. It was each individual's perception of me based on my physical appearance that dictated how I was treated. I don't know if it's the history of us as black people or if it was something that the individual had personally experienced. Whatever it was, I would become a victor or a villain.

I went above and beyond to be nice to people, hoping they would see beyond the physical and just like me. I found it difficult to tell people no, all because I didn't want them to say those oh-so-hurtful words that I heard way too often, "She think she all that." That couldn't have been further from the truth. Honestly, I didn't think very much of myself at all. My life experiences sent me mixed messages. The people who were supposed to love and protect me punished me because I was beautiful, while strangers praised me for the exact same reason. I was so confused.

Beauty was a heavy burden to carry, because for me guilt was part of the package. I was made to feel bad, ashamed and inadequate, all because of the way God created me. As a result, I found ways to downplay my physical beauty, by intentionally wearing less-than-attractive clothes and making my hair appear kinkier than it really was. I did whatever it took to fit in and not stand out. I just wanted to be liked and not judged based solely on what people could see.

It took me a lot of years and a lot of tears to be comfortable in my own skin. This wasn't because I didn't like who I was, but because I was hurt. Here I was judged, resented, disliked and abused, just because I was "beautiful."

As a grown woman, I still deal with the same nonsense. Women can be so mean and competitive. The instant an attractive female enters the room, we start to dissect her, pointing out every little flaw. Why do we do that to each other? Because of our own insecurities or feelings of inadequacy, we try to break her down to build ourselves up. It is ridiculous, but true. We are really hurting and transferring our pain to the "beautiful" female who appears to have it all. She's too cute, too sharp, too educated and has it too together.

I remember someone really close to me asking me sarcastically, "Why is it that when I walk into a room everyone likes me, but when you walk into a room no one likes you?" Those were very hurtful words that I will never forget, but I had to stop and ask myself why that was the case. What I know now is that it's not personal. If you don't like me the instant you lay eyes on me, the problem is you, not me.

Ladies, knowing yourself, loving yourself and accepting yourself is everything. God made you exactly the way you are supposed to be. No matter the shade of your skin, color of your eyes, coarseness of your hair or the thickness of your waist, celebrate you. God didn't answer my prayers to make me invisible because I'm supposed to be here. I'm supposed to be seen, I'm supposed to stand out and I'm supposed to be beautiful. Thank you, Jesus.

Don't think that because she's beautiful
she's got it easy.
The pretty girls actually have it the hardest.
The curse of being attractive means
attracting more distractions.

More men that care more about
how she looks than how she feels.
More "girlfriends" that use her beauty for their benefit.
She spends more time trying to figure out
who's around because she looks good
or because she might be a good look.

Being beautiful is a gift and a curse.
She has to be beautiful enough
to not be talked about by the other beautiful girls.
But not so beautiful that she pisses anyone else off.

Because when you're beautiful,
sometimes the hate is just as real as the love is.

@justmike_

Credit:

Reid Jr., M. E. [Just Mike]. (personal communication,
2013). Untitled. [Facebook timeline].

NOTES

I Wish I Woulda Knew Me Back Then

Elizabeth Meyette

Poet, blogger and believer in dreams-come-true, Elizabeth Meyette's journey has taken her through a career in education to a career in writing. She earned a Bachelor of Science in Education, a Master of Arts in Education and a Master of Arts in Library Science/Media/Technology from Central Michigan University. Elizabeth put her first novel, *Love's Destiny*, on the shelf for 30 years while she taught English, Journalism and Library Science/Technology in Midland Public Schools.

Upon retiring from teaching, she dusted off *Love's Destiny*, polished it and submitted it to Crimson Romance, an imprint of F&W Media, who published it in June 2012. Unlike her first novel, the sequel, *Love's Spirit*, took only seven months from inception to submission, and was published in April 2013. To coin a friend's phrase, she didn't retire, she "refired," and loves her second career as a writer. Her latest novel, *The Cavanaugh House*, is a mystery set in the Finger Lakes region of Upstate New York. She has also published poetry and freelance articles.

Elizabeth's current unpublished projects include a play, a chapbook of poetry and three children's books: *The Go-to-Sleep Tree*, *Rise and Shine, Caroline* and *At Annie's House*.

Elizabeth and her husband, Richard, live in the Great Lakes Bay area of Michigan. They have an agreement that she cannot cook on writing days after he endured burnt broccoli and overcooked chicken too many times. Fortunately, Richard is an excellent cook.

Visit Elizabeth at www.elizabethmeyette.com. Her blog, *Meyette's Musings* can be found at http://elizabethmeyette.blogspot.com.

I ONCE WAS BLIND
Elizabeth Meyette

They were the first new family on our street since before I was born.

Our neighborhood of three-story city homes that snuggled next to each other on neat lots was tree-covered with big yards. We all knew each other and adults looked out for — and disciplined — every child. While we were free to roam in all yards, we'd better not get caught picking the McAlpine's pears or the Huberth's apples without permission.

Our block overflowed with kids, and summer evenings found us all playing tag or baseball until the sun went down, when we would switch to "Ghost" and scare ourselves silly. Life was safe and predictable and good.

Having new neighbors was a novel thing in our stable little world. My best friends Ellen and Mary lived next door and behind me, respectively. Ellen and I had grown up together since birth, and Mary moved in when we were in first grade.

When I was 13 years old, the Leach family moved in two doors down. Old Mr. Myers had finally followed his wife to their heavenly resting place, which left their home vacant. The Leach family tumbled into the house in autumn after school had started. I had watched as they moved in their belongings, and I knew there was a daughter around my age.

Since I went to the Catholic grade school across the street and the Leach kids went to the public school a few blocks away, the only way to meet them was to go to their home.

I felt a little shy walking up the porch steps to their front door, wondering if someone inside was watching my progress. Ringing the bell, I felt like running like we often did at night playing "Ding and Ditch," as if no one in the neighborhood would know it was us. My feet itched to take off and speed back to my house two doors away, but suddenly the door opened and before me stood a slender teenage boy with long brown hair that fell into his eyes.

"Hi," I said.

"Hi," he answered.

Not schooled in proper new neighbor greetings, I felt awkward and my mouth was so dry that I was afraid to speak for fear a squawk would come out instead of words. I coughed a little, and feeling braver, finally spoke.

"I'm Betty. I live two doors down and I wanted to, well, say hi ... and welcome."

The 17-year-old boy squinted at me, the way smokers do when their cigarette smoke gets in their eyes. He didn't speak.

I shifted uncomfortably.

"Is your sister here?"

He nodded slightly and then closed the door, leaving it a bit ajar. Turning, I looked at the street I knew so well. I felt like Scout Finch from *To Kill a Mockingbird* when she reflected on how differently things looked from Boo Radley's porch. My familiar street did indeed look different from this vantage point, and scenes that were so familiar to me were at altered angles and perspectives.

The door reopened, interrupting my thoughts, and a 15-year-old girl a couple of inches taller than me stood there smiling.

"Hi. Jeff told me you wanted to see me."

"Yeah. Hi." Shyness suddenly crept over me again, and I doubted my confidence in taking on the role of my street's Welcome Wagon. "I'm Betty. I live two doors down." I felt the flush in my face and knew it was beet red. "I just wanted to say hi … and, um, welcome."

"Hi, Betty. I'm Tracy Leach. Come on in."

Smiling wider, she opened the screen door in invitation. Their house was in shambles and I figured it was because they had just moved in. Clothes and other belongings were strewn about on furniture, floors and stairways. Tracy took me into the kitchen and offered me a soda.

As we sat at the table, I noticed it wasn't just her height that indicated her two years' seniority; her body was amply developed and she wore makeup. My mother had said no makeup until I was in high school, so I was burning for the next year to arrive when I would be a freshman. The cosmetics counter had better be prepared!

While we talked, her brother Jeff wandered in smoking a cigarette. This was no big deal because everyone in my family smoked, including my 17-year-old brother. Everyone but me, that is. Sure, I had tried it out in the Three Sisters' Woods behind the boys' high school, but I never became a smoker.

Actually, my group of friends and I were really good kids. We got into occasional mischief, like the time Mary and I went bowling when we were 10 years old. After bowling one game we erased the score sheet and bowled another, only intending to pay for the first. Little did we know that the owner had a mechanical frame counter that kept track of every time we bowled. He read us the riot act and said he was going to call our parents unless we paid for both games. We scrabbled together enough money to pay and headed home in terror. It wasn't until many years later that it dawned on me that the owner didn't know our names and certainly didn't know our parents. But I confessed the whole incident to Mom, who grounded me and gave me extra household chores.

That incident, and smoking in the woods were probably two of my biggest offenses. As I said, we were good kids. Maybe even nerdy, although in our circle of friends we were the popular girls who were chosen as cheerleaders, which was high status at our K-8th grade school.

Anyway, Tracy and I hit it off and agreed to hang out the next day. When I returned home for supper and told Mom that I had gone over there and met her, Mom hit the roof.

"You are not to hang around with her, Betty," she said, pointing at me with the spoon she was using to stir the sauce. "You stay away."

Shocked doesn't come close to how I felt as I looked at my mother's angry face. She was the most accepting, inviting, nonjudgmental person I knew. All my friends called her "Mom." In fact, everyone who came to our house did. Our house was a haven for anyone in need of a place to be for a while. This was totally uncharacteristic of her.

"Mom, Tracy is nice. Why can't I hang out with her?"

"You stay away." She returned to her cooking, her back indicating that the conversation was over.

"But, Mom …"

She turned and gave me that you-don't-want-to-mess-with-me look. I slunk off to the living room to watch TV with Dad.

Against my mother's orders, I did hang out with Tracy the next day. She seemed so nice, and I could not understand my mother's dislike of her. We continued to hang out, and one time I took Tracy to Mary's to meet my group of friends.

We always gathered at one of our houses to listen to music, talk about boys, and get makeup tips from Donna and Sue, who were already allowed to wear makeup. They would generously share their stash and apply it to our faces with strict instructions on what brush to use, what angle to hold it at and how much makeup to apply so the white lipstick and blue eye shadow looked "natural" and not overdone.

With Tracy there this time, I seemed to see my friends through different eyes. They seemed young, like little girls playing dress-up. Tracy already knew how to apply makeup and used it copiously. Instead of pale eye shadow and thin liner, her eyes were heavily drawn with dark shadow, black liner and a liberal application of mascara. She was quiet as she watched us and did not take part in our fun at all. I knew she thought my friends were childish, and I knew they did not approve of her.

My hope for drawing Tracy into my group of friends was a complete failure. My soul was divided between loyalty and love for my friends and a new feeling of disdain for them. It was as if I had a completely different view of them as I sat beside Tracy trying to make this work. I knew this would fast become a choice for me — my lifelong friends or this new girl that I so fiercely wanted to protect from all these people who were judging her.

As I got to know Tracy more, I became aware that she smoked, because I could smell it on her clothing. I also suspected, though I had no proof, that evenings she went out with her brother were spent in activities foreign to me. And although some time had passed, their house never did get cleaned up and, in fact, continued to get messier.

Now, I didn't feel right judging that, because our house was chaotic and messy with kids all around and friends in and out at all hours. Mom was many wonderful things, but housekeeper did not top the list. Our dishes were done every day and our clothes were clean. Food was put away and trash was taken out. However, furniture was dusty and beds weren't always made. Toys were sometimes left where they had been played with, but overall it was healthy. At the Leach house, it was a different kind of messy. Food was left out, trash overflowed and there were odors of dirty clothes. I turned a blind eye.

I saw Tracy and her brother Jeff walking away down the street one evening and as they passed a yard, Tracy dropped something on the grass. My stomach felt sick. Surely I hadn't seen that. I waited a while and then walked down to the yard. Lying in a pile of rubble were a crumpled cigarette pack, an old tissue and a used sanitary napkin. I had a sick feeling thinking that this might have been what Tracy dropped. Doubts that had been forming in my brain gripped me and wouldn't let go. But somehow that made me more determined to protect her. If she was around people like me and my friends, she would change and become a "good kid" too. It's called "Savior Syndrome" and it often brings heartache.

Because we went to different schools and because New York winters keep people inside a lot, my interactions with Tracy tapered off. It was basketball season and my friends and I were busy with cheerleading practice and games. Also, it was nearing the end of my eighth grade year. We were getting ready to move on to high school and taking entrance exams and applying for scholarships.

Another phenomenon had entered my life and captured my attention at that time — my first steady boyfriend. I wanted to spend every minute with David, so my focus on defying my mother and hanging out with Tracy waned. We didn't see much of each other for several months, but I still felt an inexplicable loyalty to her. Perhaps because everyone else was against her, I felt I was her champion.

I still saw Tracy once in a while, but something within me began to recognize that Mom and my friends were right. My inner moral compass knew that the disdain I'd felt for my friends was unjustified; they were my friends because we were so much alike. I couldn't judge them without judging myself. And how could my mother, a woman so accepting of everyone, not accept this family who lived just two doors down?

One spring morning when I went downstairs to breakfast, my mother sat beside me and took my hand.

"I have some bad news, honey," she said.

A chill ran through me and I looked at the morning newspaper folded in her lap. My eyes met hers and saw how they glistened with tears. "It's Tracy. She died in a car accident last night. I don't know if you want to see this."

I looked at the newspaper and nodded. My whole body started to shake as tears burned my eyes.

Mom unfolded the paper and a banner headline read, "Teens Killed in Crash During Car Chase." The large photo showed a car crumpled against a tree. There were no bodies in the picture.

Reading the article, my brain refused to make sense of it. Tracy and another boy and girl had been out joyriding when a policeman tried to pull them over for speeding. They took off and the chase reached speeds of 100 miles per hour.

I thought about Tracy. She was so full of life and fun. Was she laughing as they sped along? Was she scared? I wondered if she was in the front or back seat; the article said the boy was driving. Did she beg him to stop? Did she egg him on? With Tracy, you never knew.

My stomach lurched as I read the article. Trying to evade the police, the driver careered through streets, screeching tires and scaring others. They drove out into a rural area, speeding along a country road, the police in close pursuit. Surprised by a curve in the road, the driver swerved and the car went airborne, slamming into a tree and ejecting all three teens. One teen was alive when police arrived, but I knew it wasn't Tracy. She had been decapitated; her head had been sliced off by the impact. The other girl was pregnant. All of them dead.

My sorrow cut into my gut and tears streamed down my face. Unaware of it as I read, my mother had made me a cup of tea and set it before me as I finished the article. I looked at her through blurry vision.

"You knew. You knew she lived dangerously," I whispered.

"Yes, I knew."

"And you were trying to protect me."

She nodded.

"Mom …"

I began to sob. My mother folded me into her arms and let me cry.

Tracy's funeral was at our cathedral right across the street from my school. As I sat in history class at 11 a.m., I heard the bells begin to toll as they brought her body into the church. Each toll of the bell was like a knife through my heart. The lump in my throat hurt as I fought back sobs mourning my friend. I had wanted to skip school to attend her funeral, but my mother said no. She wanted this experience behind me and thought my place was in school, learning. I didn't learn anything at school that day. But I did learn.

I was angry at my mother for not allowing me to attend Tracy's funeral, but my anger was based in fear. I knew that part of me was afraid — I could have been in that car with Tracy at some point. My mother could have had to identify my body lying cold and still on a metal table in an autopsy room. And my mother knew that.

As I listened to the mournful bells, I realized that with Tracy, I was living on the edge. There was a darkness to her life that somehow beckoned me, a young naïve girl. While I convinced myself that I was noble because I defended Tracy from the judgment of my mother and my friends, in truth, a part of me was fascinated by the life I suspected she led, so different from my own experience.

It took many years for me to understand and accept why my mother forbade me to hang out with Tracy. And it took many years for me to acknowledge that my disobedience was not only dangerous, but disrespectful to Mom. Had I continued to hang out with Tracy, I would have alienated all of my friends, and perhaps started down a road to my own destruction. It's hard to admit that I was wrong. My 13-year-old judgment was no match for my mother's wisdom and my friends' instincts.

This was a time in my life when I thought I had all of the answers. This was a time when I felt like I would live forever and that I possessed the wisdom of the ages. "Hubris" is a word that describes one who has so much pride that she thinks she is smarter than anyone, and overestimates what she is capable of doing or understanding. Hubris means thinking she has all of the answers. Oh man, I was so full of hubris. It was humbling to realize that I didn't know everything. Whatever my mother saw about Tracy that I was blind to was based on her wisdom and life experience. Whatever my friends picked up on about Tracy that I refused to see was instinctual self-preservation.

Am I proud of what I did in this instance? I'm proud that I was willing to stand up for an underdog, someone others rejected. But I am not proud of my refusal to see that Tracy was making choices contrary to my value system. I am not proud that I disobeyed my mother, or that I judged my friends so harshly.

This Betty, the one who writes this today, would like to say the following to 13-year-old Betty:

"I wish I woulda known you then. I like who you are. I like your kindness in the face of a difficult situation. But, girl, you'd better get your head on straight! Listen to those who love you. You surround yourself with people who are kind, with people who share your values. There is a reason for that. Deep down, your heart knows what it needs — the loving support of people who truly care about you. Cherish your wise mother. Cherish your true friends. But most of all, listen to the truth in your heart. You saw the danger all along."

My wish for you, dear reader, beautiful young lady, is that you, too, will listen to the wise ones in your life and that you will listen to the truth your heart speaks to you. God bless you.

NOTES

I Wish I Woulda Knew Me Back Then

Veronica Rice

Veronica Rice was raised in Flint, Michigan, and currently resides in Miami, Florida. She attended the Detroit College of Business and the University of Miami and is employed by What Matters Films.

In her spare time, Ms. Rice is active in the New Birth RAJ Dance ministry and New Birth Loves Kitchen Ministry. Veronica is also involved in the Kids in Distress Bike Challenge and the Quantum Zero Speed Cycling Team.

Quotes Veronica lives by are "I walk by faith, not by sight," and "Prayer can change things."

MY CROSS TO BEAR
Veronica Rice

As a young girl growing up in a small town in Arkansas, I can vaguely recall a few moments with my dad. What I do know is that I loved him so very much and wanted to spend time with him as much as possible. The few times that I do remember were happy times, just because my daddy wanted to be with his little girl. Those happy times for me were spent at the horse racetrack and at the county line liquor store.

As a little girl of about 5 or 6, I knew something was wrong with this picture. I realized that the man I loved so much had two problems. One was gambling and the other was drinking. Despite the conflict, those moments at the horse track and county line were my happiest. Some may ask, "How could that have been happy?" Well, those were the only times I recall being with him. I admit I don't have any memories of going to the park, playing doll house or going to get ice cream like most kids. But I wanted to be daddy's little girl, so whatever time and how it was spent did not matter, because I was with my daddy.

Things may have been a bit different had my mom known where he was taking me. She would have flipped out and never let me go again, so I kept quiet.

Although it was a small town, there were still problems. For the most part, though, I felt free as a child. I climbed trees, chucked rocks and ate a lot of junk food from the café on the hill. Life was good. Well that's how most would perceive it.

About the mid- to late 70s, things began to become dark and dim in our lives. My mom, a strong woman, was faced with making some major decisions regarding herself and her four children. Those happy moments I spoke about earlier with my dad became no more and the place that was my home and safe haven became hell. For many years, that was my life. This is my story and my cross to bear.

    During that time, my mom was married to my stepdad, and though I have asked the Lord to forgive me, I did not like the man much. He was not a loving, caring person in my eyes at all. To me, he was mean and evil with no care or compassion for anyone but himself. Yeah, I could almost say I hated the man.

    I can remember there was a time when my stepdad moved us to Texas. We did not live there very long, but I recall him still being as mean as ever. Nothing had changed in my eyes. It seemed to have gotten worse. At this time, I lived in terror, which I kept hidden. I honestly believed that my stepdad did not care much for me because of who my real dad was. Since he did not like my dad, I was targeted. Every time he would come into a room — it did not matter if it was occupied with my entire family — I was terrified. It was so bad that my hair would fall out. I was always nervous, looking out of the corner of my eyes trying to see where he was. I lived in complete terror.

I remember being taunted, because he knew I was afraid of him and was watching his every move. He would sometimes jump out at me to scare me. I guess in his sick little mind he thought it was funny, but I knew he was doing it purposely to frighten me. It worked, because I was completely afraid and did not want to be left alone with him at all. I was humiliated for years and did not understand why. What did I do to deserve this?

Just when I thought it could not get any worse, it did. I remember sitting at the dinner table eating some chicken. When I became full, just like any other child would do, I threw the rest away. Well, that completely pissed him off to the point where he made me eat the chicken out of the garbage. All I can remember was that I was so afraid that I did whatever I could to eat that chicken out of the trash. I was gagging the whole time, but was determined to eat it, because I did not know what he would do if I didn't.

Can you imagine making a child eat from the trash and watching her gag and vomit trying to continue to eat? Who does that? I knew as a child that eating from the trash was not good. Trash is for trash.

I kept that secret bottled up for years, never telling anyone, because I felt embarrassed, afraid and alone. I never told my mother about these things either, because if she had known, she would probably have spent some serious time behind bars. There was no way

I was going to have that happen. No one knew for years, not even my three older brothers.

Many years had passed and it came to the point when my mother had enough. I remember that day very well. It was around the late 70s, maybe 1978. My mother was tired of the mistreatment that she suffered and made up in her mind that she was done. She packed up all she could in one suitcase that looked like a chest. Y'all know that old school suitcase with the padlock that was so heavy you had to almost use a forklift to pick it up. Somehow, she managed to put all we had in it. She sent my brothers ahead with my uncle to Ohio and she and I came shortly after.

I will never forget that Greyhound bus ride to Columbus.

It was long, hot and smelly. My mom and I had the "pleasure" of sitting in front of this unpleasant, inconsiderate man who felt the need to take his shoes off and rest his smelly feet in between the headrest of our seats on the bus. Lawd, have mercy, I still remember that awful smell. It was like smelling musk, vomit, roadkill and corn chips combined. There was no way we could ride smelling that mess, and changing seats was not an option since the bus was full.

So my mother, being the supermom, rose to the occasion and sprayed her most expensive perfume — back in the day it was Jean-Naté — all over his feet to mask the horrible smell. I thank God for my mother, because as uncomfortable as that long ride was, she did what was necessary to make it comfortable for me. That's what mothers do.

To fast forward things a bit, I can say that life is a challenge and full of choices. I must admit, I've had a lot of challenges, but I can't go into detail about all of them. I've also made a lot of bad choices in my life.

The year was around 1989, when this strong, handsome young man stole my heart. Actually, we had known each other for many years, grew up together and dated previously. This time around, the relationship had become serious.

I had just graduated from high school and felt like I had kept my boyfriend waiting long enough, and figured it was the perfect time for us to become one. At the time I felt it was okay because we had discussed getting married and everything. As I look back now, waiting should have been the only option. However, that was the choice I made.

My sisters, I can tell you this: never rush into any relationship based on sex or the flesh. You will be disappointed every time. As women, we become vulnerable when we give away our most precious gift and when we are rejected, it tears away at our very soul.

So my sisters, always pray and wait on God to give you an answer. More importantly, if you don't have an answer from the Lord, that means to continue to wait patiently. Remember that time spent waiting is not time wasted. The one thing that we fail horribly in is waiting. We want things in our time. When you wait on the Lord, it will save you a lot of grief and pain. Isaiah 40:31 (KJV) states, "But they that wait upon the LORD shall renew their strength; they shall mount up with wings as eagles; they shall run, and not be weary; and they shall walk and not faint."

Around 2010, I received a call from a number that I did not recognize, so of course I let it go to voicemail. When I checked my messages, it was kind of funny, because the person did not know if he was really leaving a message. But before hanging up, the person said, "This is your daddy." Oh my goodness! Did I just hear right? When I heard that, I almost fainted. It was my dad. I was overwhelmed with excitement and emotions. It had been over 20 years since I'd seen my dad and over 10 years since I'd heard from him.

After I got myself together, I decided I would call the next day since it was late. My heart was racing with the anticipation of being able to talk to my dad. I wanted to know everything. I had so many unanswered questions. Would I be ready for this? What would I say? What would he say? Then I became nervous about the whole situation, but felt like it was time to clear the air of any tension between us.

I called and a pleasant woman answered the phone, so I politely introduced myself and immediately felt her excitement. She then proceeded to tell me she was my dad's wife and how happy she was to hear from me. Our conversation was brief but very nice.

Then the big moment arrived. My daddy came to the phone, and let me tell you, when I heard his voice, I was so happy. It was like a weight had been lifted off my shoulders. At that point, nothing else mattered. I had my daddy back in my life again.

We talked and he apologized for not being a part of my life for so many years. That was all I needed to hear. Nothing else needed to be said or discussed as far as I was concerned. I never stopped loving my dad, and I had forgiven him a long time ago.

With that phone call, I was at peace.

During the conversation, I learned that I had other siblings and a few nieces and nephews. Wow! I had a whole new family I knew nothing about. God willing, I would have the opportunity to meet and get to know each of them.

I was at a point in my life where I put my faith and trust in God. I put my burdens on Him, and even forgave my stepdad and anyone else who had ever caused me pain. We can't change the past, but we can trust and believe God for a better tomorrow.

We all have to realize that life is so precious, and holding past grudges and unforgiveness takes away from the enjoyment of life. God did not intend for us to live that way. He wants us to live a life with Him being the main focus. If there's anything else that's troubling us, He will fix it if we just give it to Him. Our Lord and Savior Jesus Christ forgives us, so who are we not to forgive others? Think about that.

Life has a way of teaching you what's really important. For me, my relationship with Jesus Christ and His plan for my life, spending quality time with family and friends and helping others is what matters.

My advice to you is to be encouraged. We all have trials and tribulations, but don't allow them to hinder you from what God has already purposed in your life. 1Peter 2:9 (NIV) says, "But you are a chosen people, a royal priesthood, a holy nation, God's special possession, that you may declare the praises of him who called you out of darkness into his wonderful light." This is who you are when you become a child of God.

Some people ask if I would change anything about my life. I'm not sure I would, because I believe everything happens for a reason, and my experiences have made me into a woman of faith and an extra-ordinary woman of God.

I'm a work in progress and don't know everything, but I have learned that Jesus has been the answer to everything in my life. I've made a commit-ment to serve Him with my whole heart. I'm not perfect and may make mistakes along the way. But with a sincere, humble heart I pray and ask God to forgive me and help me not repeat those mistakes.

Don't worry about the past or what people say or do. Always put your trust in God and He will be with you in your time of need. When you have a personal relationship with Jesus, you will find peace in His promises, which are in the Word of God.

I truly believe God has a great work for me to do as well as all of you. Let's step out on faith and trust God for what He has promised. I encourage all of you to go to God in prayer and spend time in His Word. I guarantee He will show you great and mighty things.

My prayer is that my testimony will be an encouragement to someone who may be struggling with their life choices. This was just a small testimony, but to God be the glory. I encourage you to accept Christ into your life because He will never leave or forsake you. When you can't find your way, Jesus will direct your path.

I thank you Lord, for allowing me to be a testimony to others and that you get the glory out of everything that I say and do. Amen to the Father, Son and Holy Spirit.

NOTES

KeanaMonique Smith

KeanaMonique is a Pontiac, Michigan native, and graduated from Pontiac Northern High School. She's a mother of a smart 14-year-old son named Jayce, who was born deaf, and the two of them communicate with American Sign Language.

Upon graduation, Ms. Smith furthered her education in medical assisting and law enforcement, and ultimately found her passion in the beauty industry as an expert in manicuring. Specializing in acrylic nails, manicures and pedicures, nail art etc., she was determined to be successful in her newfound passion and became the owner of her own nail salon, N'Chanted Nails.

KeanaMonique has a passion in helping others and making a difference in their lives, whether big or small. In 2012, she had the opportunity to become a bone marrow donor to someone she had never met. The two of them keep in contact frequently and have become good friends.

Ms. Smith enjoys writing poetry, traveling, reading and spending time with family and close friends.

ADDICTED
KeanaMonique Smith

Everyone has an addiction.

My addiction was driven by attention I was lacking during a crucial time in my life. The addiction, in more ways than one, impaired my judgment and forced me to see things that weren't actually there, almost like hallucinating when you are on a high caused by heroin. Heroin is a powerful drug that has ruined many lives. For the fortunate, some heroin addicts were able to quit with some assistance from programs, friends or loved ones. Others quit using the cold turkey method, which allows you to go through withdrawal from the drug, causing physical, mental and emotional distress and other issues.

Here is my story to free myself from a heroin substitute. Although it's not an actual drug, I'm sure you'll understand when I'm finished telling you my story.

My name is Isis, and I was addicted to DeVaughn Davis.

As if I'm not already dealing with enough bullshit at home, I'm four months pregnant and I don't know where his daddy is. Niggas be on some other type of shit. They wanna talk all good, lay up, get down, get dressed and disappear. I swear, if you ever wanna see a

113

nigga disappear, tell him you're pregnant. It's almost like the government got a space on earth, like a witness protection plan for niggas running from responsibility. It's as if there's a sign on all the expressways for the niggas running from their future baby mommas. I swear it's gotta read something like this.

"IF YOU OR ANYONE YOU KNOW HAS A CHILD ON THE WAY AND YOU'RE NOT READY TO BE A FATHER, CALL 1-800-NOT-MINE."

Oh well, I'm good, I'll take care of my child with or without him. I'm 19 and the job I have has full benefits. I'll be fine. Off to work I go.

As I walked back into my job, I must have seen the finest man I've seen in a long time. He was sitting there in the lobby on his cell phone. I guess I can try to flirt, I thought. I ain't showing yet, so let me see if I still got it. Being pregnant, my skin was flawless and my hair was real long and healthy. I knew from the man's point of view, I had to be in the top selected few to still have a boyfriend on my team. I had a good job, nice car, and my own crib. I like to think that Neyo wrote those two songs for me, "I love her 'cause she got her own," and "Miss Independent." Yeah, those are my theme songs.

As I walked past him, we made eye contact, and that's when it all started. I walked toward the back to punch back in and hollered at my homegirl Red, "Girl, did you see that sexy nigga in the lobby?"

She replied, "You must be talking about D. Dave. Yeah, I saw him, but he ain't shit. I know him from back in the day, when he was always hanging around my brothers, trying to be one of the big dogs."

I said, "Oh, OK, that's what's up, good looking out."

We laughed and I went to pull my next chart. I guess it might've been meant for me to know who this "ain't-shit nigga" was, because his chart was next in line. DeVaughn Davis was the name on the chart, so I opened the door and called his name. "Mr. Davis." We made eye contact again and he got up and came to the back with me. I swear I was instantly put in a trance, because he had the most beautiful hazel eyes I had seen on a guy. Now I've seen females with hazel eyes, but never had I seen them on a guy. Instant red flag, but I didn't pay it any attention.

As I proceeded to take him to the nurses' station to get his vitals, I learned he was there for an injury on the job. I introduced myself and followed the proper protocol to get him prepped to see the doctor. With on-the-job injuries, patients have to have a drug screen. Immediately, I assumed he was dirty, because he just appeared like the type to smoke weed. Yeah, I was profiling, but in my field you had to be cautious of who you were dealing with. Not that his weed consumption had anything to do with me, I guess I was just being nosey. I handed him a cup and told him to give me some urine and I drew a line on the cup. I also told him that his company required screened urine collections, to assure that it was in fact his urine.

Sometimes I wish I was a man, just to see what he was working with. Being pregnant had my hormones on 10, and I was ready to get it in, but I still had to remain professional. I advised him that he would need someone to go in with him, and unfazed, he said, "OK."

As I waited for the two of them to return, I went to find Red and told her that I was about to see if I still had it, and get my flirt on. She shook her head and said, "Leave that beast with the hazel eyes alone." Another red flag, but I didn't pay it any attention. As much as I wanted to flirt, I remained cool and did my job. I directed him to his room, told him to strip down and put on the blue shorts, and the doctor would be in shortly.

After a while, I heard a page overhead. "Isis to the doctors' station, Isis to the doctors' station."

As I got there, Dr. Shelton told me to give Mr. Davis a lumbar spine 5-view X-ray. Again, I was trying to be professional but I kept being put with this dude, so I assumed it was meant for us to communicate. I did the X-ray with minimal to no talking, as hard as it was. Do you know what it's like to be alone in a room with a dude that is cut up, smelling good, and sexy? I instantly got turned on. But I knew I had to shake it off. I showed him back to his room, and that was that.

Later on that day, I got a phone call from Red, telling me that the dude from work was inquiring about me. She said her brother told her to get my number for

DeVaughn, 'cause he was checking for me. I declined the offer and told her if he wanted my number he had to get it himself.

The next day was a Saturday, and I figured I'd go to the mall after my doctor's visit to buy my son some clothes before he made his grand entrance. As I was walking through the mall with my head down, I looked up and guess who was standing right in front of me? DeVaughn. We exchanged small talk and as I proceeded to walk away, he called my name, told me to call him, and gave me his number. As hard as it was to keep from smiling, I said I'd think about it, because I had other things on my plate that might prevent me from calling him.

He asked what they were and I said, "None of your business," and walked away.

I must admit I said to myself, Yeah, I still got it. Then I looked down at my stomach and rubbed it, and said, "Yeah lil fella, yo momma still got it."

About two weeks had passed and it was time for DeVaughn's recheck at work. When I saw his name, I skipped over the chart, not wanting to seem anxious to talk to or see him. So Red grabbed the chart and called him back. They talked for a second and he was put in his room. She came to me and said, "He wants to talk to you," and before she put his room number on the board for the doctors, I went into the room to see what he wanted.

Surprisingly, he told me that he did a little research and he knew my first and last name, where I lived, and the last thing he revealed was that he knew I was pregnant. I asked him why he felt it was necessary to do a background investigation on me. He said when he wants something, he gets it. So I said to him, "If I'm what you want then you gotta come better than a background investigation to get me, starting now." I closed the door, and just stood there for a minute. Then I said, "Game on." I put the room number on the board and went on about my day.

From then on, he must have been on 10 with his flattery, because I was getting roses, chocolates and anything else I could possibly think of that could be delivered. Yeah, I was being pulled in with trickery. I call it trickery because I didn't know it then, but all the things he was doing to me were an overplay for the underplay.

By this time, I was about seven months pregnant and I still hadn't had sex. I was getting frustrated every day because I wanted to have sex, but didn't know what to do about it. Of course I masturbated, but I wanted to be held, kissed, touched, caressed and everything else that came along with lovemaking. I couldn't necessarily call it lovemaking, because I didn't love him, but there was a strong sense of lust.

One night I got up enough courage to call him. We must have talked for hours, as if we were in high school. We talked as the sun rose, and we talked through the setting of the same. It seemed as if I had known him for a long time. It just felt right. I mean, it just felt *right*.

But still I refused to sleep with him. That's until the doctor told me that having sex was okay. Even though I was uneasy about sleeping with DeVaughn while I was pregnant, my hormones were outta control. So I decided to take it there and give in. At the time, I was totally unaware of the slipup I was about to make. All I knew was I wanted to have that orgasm I was chasing.

I had planned the perfect evening. I purchased some sexy maternity lingerie and I had soft music playing and candles lit. DeVaughn came over, but for whatever reason he was upset. I'm not sure what was wrong, but he wasn't the same person. I began to massage his shoulders to attempt to relieve the tension and get his mind off of whatever had been troubling him.

We began kissing and touching and before I knew it, he was on top of me. The way he touched me sent a jolt of electricity through my body, awakening my inner freak. It was almost as if I had been resurrected by the prince of passion. His kisses weren't too wet or too dry, but just right. The way his tongue waited to be invited into my mouth was just pleasing to me. Every time he touched, kissed or even breathed on me, he excited my juice box. He caressed each of my very full breasts, kissing and sucking on them ever so gently.

By this time, I was ready for him to enter my secret place. He started to travel down the road no man had gone since the night I conceived. Of course, I must admit I was scared, but the need for this release was so overwhelming it had to be captured. I felt like a heroin addict taking her first hit. He was my drug and I immediately became addicted.

From that moment, DeVaughn and I were inseparable; we did everything together. Although my son wasn't his, he took me to meet his family, and introduced me as his "future." We laughed, but his mother didn't find it funny. It didn't bother me at that point, but what did bother me was when she said, "If that's your future, then that must mean Felicia is the past?" If looks could kill, the look DeVaughn shot his mother would've killed her right there in the living room. Now Felicia was a name I hadn't heard before. But I didn't take heed to the hidden message at that time.

After that, he was instantly ready to leave. Since he drove, we left. I never asked who Felicia was, I just made a mental note. It wasn't like Felicia was an uncommon name, so for me to ask around about a Felicia, I needed more to go on. He was still my "boo thang" though, and I just tucked the name Felicia under my hat. I guess at that point I began to somewhat pay attention to signs. Not totally, but somewhat. On the way back home, DeVaughn's cell phone was blowing up and the more they called, the more irritated he became. To this day, I never found out who was calling, but I can only imagine it was Felicia.

One day, while I was at home preparing for my baby shower, I got an unexpected phone call. The number on my phone was a number that I didn't recognize, so I answered it. The voice on the other end belonged to a woman, and she asked for me, so I told her that I was who she was asking for. She proceeded to tell me that she and DeVaughn had just finished having sex, and to prove she wasn't lying, he had on blue drawers. I told her I had more important things to attend to than to worry about who she was letting put miles on her pussy. I ended the phone call, but I stored the number under who I presumed to be Felicia. I waited a little while, then I called DeVaughn and told him I needed help putting together my son's baby bed. He said he'd be right over.

When he got there, he had a look on his face that made him appear so relaxed. I told him I wanted to get down, and he hesitantly obliged my request. I only said that to really see if his drawers were blue. We began to get it in, and when I saw the color of his underwear I instantly got sick. The fact that I said I wasn't feeling good didn't bother him because I was so far along in my pregnancy. He let me lie down and asked me if I needed anything. I told him I was fine, that I just wanted to go to sleep. He left my house and for the rest of the day, I never heard from him. I knew right then that the woman on the phone wasn't lying.

The next day, I called my cousin Danielle and asked her if she could find some proof that DeVaughn was messing around with Felicia. She told me to give her about an hour and she would call me back. I told her not to play, but get to work.

Danielle called me back within 30 minutes and gave me the rundown on Felicia. She gave me her phone number, where she lived, worked, the kind of car she drove and other information I didn't even ask her to get. But the last thing she told me was that Felicia and DeVaughn were definitely a couple. They broke up often, but always got back together. She even told me that DeVaughn and Felicia were like the modern day Ike and Tina. She said that DeVaughn was known for putting the smack down on females, and if I didn't believe her I could call her friend Tiffany, who used to date DeVaughn.

I took the number, but insisted on having Danielle call her on the three-way. I didn't wanna just call her out of the blue asking about her past, since she didn't know me. Danielle told me to push the mute button while she called Tiffany.

I listened with so much intensity, hoping that Danielle was wrong in her findings. I heard out of her own mouth how she and DeVaughn would get into verbal arguments and he would hit her. She even began to cry as she was telling Danielle some of the stories of how she was choked, beaten and other grotesque details of how he belittled her and made her do things she was strongly against. She mentioned how one time he made her suck his dick in front of his friends, to prove how much she loved him. She said she didn't want to do it, but because he was already hitting her, she felt she had no choice. After she finished, he forced her to suck everybody else's dick in the room. Talk about the ultimate disrespect. She even said that he forced himself on her anally and described how she lost control of her bowels because of the amount of force he used.

At that moment I became extremely nauseous, and I didn't want to hear anymore, so I disconnected. I didn't mention it to him, at least not then, because I wasn't sure how he would react.

I decided to take the next few days to focus on the baby shower and the arrival of my son. After about four days, I got a knock on the door, and it was DeVaughn. He had bags from Macy's, Polo, Nautica, and the Baby Gap. He said he played the numbers in the streets and hit, and since I was his "future," he decided to buy my son and me a few gifts. With my conscience being clouded by material things, I overlooked the "Tiffany" conversation I heard a few days earlier, accepted the gifts and went on with the regularly scheduled program.

In the back of my mind, I couldn't dismiss Tiffany's voice when she mentally revisited her past with DeVaughn. I just figured it was possible that people can change.

Up until then, I never mentioned my family to DeVaughn, but I figured it might be time to introduce him to my mother. I called her and told her I wanted her to meet someone. She told me to bring him over.

My mother has a strong relationship with God and prays about everything, from what she should eat, to what she should wear. She believes that God will direct her in every aspect of her life.

When we got to my mother's house, she was standoffish, but still polite. I knew she saw or felt something, but didn't say anything at that time. Later on that night, my mother called me and told me that she'd been in constant prayer about DeVaughn and she didn't like the feeling she was getting. She even told me to be careful, but never said why. I just brushed it off, not paying attention to what she was telling me, by not telling me, if that makes any sense.

As my baby shower approached, I was overly excited about the fun I wanted to have. I got up and went to the spa, had a manicure and pedicure, got my hair done and picked out a cute outfit to complement my pregnant figure.

The baby shower was a huge success, and I got everything and more that I put on my registry list for my prince. As the shower began to end, I called

DeVaughn and asked him if he could meet me at the hall to help me take my gifts home. He never answered, so I got assistance from my family and friends. When I got home, I tried to call DeVaughn again, and still no answer. I showered and went to bed.

About a week later, I was starting my maternity leave. As I was in Bible study, I began to feel contractions, but I blew them off as Braxton-Hicks contractions. While I was sitting in Bible study, I received a text message from DeVaughn that read, "I miss you and want to see you."

I replied, "Same here and I'll call you when I get out of church."

Little did I know that I was in labor, since my water hadn't broken yet, but it was happening. As I walked around for the offering, the pastor said to me, "Isis, you haven't had that baby yet?"

I replied, "No, not yet."

He said, "Don't worry, it's coming faster than you think."

As I walked back to my seat, I looked at my watch and noticed that my Braxton-Hicks were real. I sat down and began to breathe deeply. I was trying to make it out of church, then head to the hospital. The pastor asked that we all stand to be dismissed, and at that moment I felt something crack, but I wasn't sure what it was. When I stood up, my water broke, with fluid gushing down my legs. I was frozen, just watching my pants get wet, as if I had urinated on myself. I screamed for my mother, and she came to get me. When she saw me, she immediately said, "It's time. I'm about to be a grandmother."

She rushed me to the hospital and we were instantly admitted to the birthing unit. As I got cleaned up and prepped for the delivery, I contacted Danielle and asked her to let my son's father know I was in labor and where I was. I knew if I called him, he wouldn't answer. She called me back and told me she spoke to him, but he said he was about to play ball, and for me to call my real baby's daddy. That tore me apart, but I had to think about it later. I had to focus on bringing a healthy baby into the world.

The labor lasted about 20 minutes and it was over. My son was here weighing in at eight pounds, 15.4 ounces. My son, whom I waited nine months for, was finally here. I named him Ryan Hezekiah Thomas.

I proceeded to call DeVaughn to tell him my son was born. When he answered, he sounded pissed off, but I was too excited to worry about what he was dealing with. I told him how much the baby weighed, and what time he was born. I was so overjoyed with emotion I began to cry. DeVaughn asked me what was wrong, and I shared with him the message my son's father had sent to me through Danielle. In his anger, or whatever it was, his words were, "Now that you're not pregnant I don't want no shit outta you."

With a confused look on my face, I was like, "Whatever."

He said, "If you think I'm playing, try me."

From that day on, my situation with DeVaughn was never the same.

After that incident, I heard what was said, but I was reluctant to listen to what he was really telling me. Maybe because I was somewhat head over heels for him, or maybe it was the fact that I thought I might've loved him. Nevertheless, I was oblivious to what was actually going on.

Life as I knew it was great. I had my son, who was, and is the joy of my life. I still had my own space and the freedom to do what I wanted. I loved motherhood, and although it was trying, it was all worth it.

At that time, Ryan was 4 weeks old, and he had to go to the doctor for his first checkup. As I was sitting in the lobby of the doctor's office, I received a text message from DeVaughn.

"Man, damn, where you at? Just drove past the crib, and you ain't there."

Puzzled, I responded, "I'm at the doctor's office."

We exchanged messages for a few minutes until I was called to the back. What happened next changed my world. As Ryan was being checked out, the doctor told me that he was growing well, to keep him on his set schedule for feeding, and to rotate milk and water bottles.

Then he pulled up a seat near me and handed me this packet of pamphlets. One of the pamphlets read, "Dealing with hearing loss." The doctor was very vague on what he was telling me. All he said was that Ryan was given an AVR test in the hospital, and he failed. I wasn't sure what AVR stood for, because he didn't offer any more information on the subject. He said to read the information and contact the number listed to schedule another test in one month. By that point, all I heard was blah, blah, blah, blah, blah, like the teacher on Charlie Brown. Nothing he said made sense to me. After that, he got up and left.

I packed Ryan up and left the doctor's office. As I headed home, all these crazy thoughts were in my head, like, What did I do during my pregnancy? Was this my fault? Can this be corrected? But most importantly, what is really wrong with my son?

Instead of going home, I went to my grandmother's house. I knew my grandmother would make all of this gibberish make sense. When I arrived and explained to her what was said, she was puzzled also. We got on the computer and Googled AVR, which stood for Audio Visual Reaction. Basically, what that means is the hospital does a series of tests on newborn babies to make sure their vision and hearing is OK. In Ryan's case, he passed the visual part but failed the auditory portion. After crying and crying and crying some more, I knew I had to pull it together for Ryan.

The time came for me to take Ryan to the ENT (ear, nose and throat) specialist. It was there they gave him a diagnosis of bilateral severe-to-profound deafness. In normal terms, that meant my son was deaf. I was 20 years old, and my first child was deaf. How was I supposed to deal with that?

On top of dealing with Ryan, and devoting all my time to doctor visits and enrolling him in school, I didn't really have much time to see DeVaughn. That pissed him off. I couldn't go back to work full time because of Ryan's hearing loss. I had to make sure he got to school two days a week. I had a 2-month-old son in school learning to use sign language, and I still had to work and maintain our living conditions. Talk about being a single parent. What made matters worse was being a single parent with a child who had a disability.

After trying to bring some normalcy to our lives, I had some serious restructuring to do. Everything revolved around teaching Ryan and learning sign language. I hadn't talked to DeVaughn in a few days and when I decided to reach out to him, it was all bad. He began to rant and rave about me not being available to him and ignoring his needs. I tried to explain what I was dealing with, but all he said was, "Damn, that's fucked up." As if I wasn't emotional enough, he started to make it about him, complaining about his needs.

As time went on, DeVaughn became verbally abusive. He would curse, yell and say all types of demeaning slurs to me.

One time, he was yelling so loudly, I asked him to quiet down. He replied, "What for? Ryan's deaf, he can't hear me." Right then I knew it was time for him to leave. I asked him to calm down and to please leave. He refused, saying, "I'm not going nowhere, I'm staying right here and you gone talk to me. I don't care what you dealing with." We argued, then he just left. Before he got all the way out of my house, he picked up a glass elephant that sat on my mantle and threw it at me. Luckily he missed.

I should have heeded the warning but I didn't, and it only got worse from there.

A few days went by and I was going on with my life as I normally did. I got a phone call from DeVaughn saying he was sorry for what he did the other night. He asked if I called the police, and I told him I didn't. Then he asked if he could come over, saying he wanted to give me something. I guess I got suckered in by the false apology and the weak tone of his voice, because I said yes.

When he got to my house, he had the exact same glass elephant that he threw and broke a few days prior. The act was kind, but the original elephant couldn't be replaced. It was given to me by someone special who had recently passed away. I accepted the gift, and the apology, and it was back to the drawing board.

We were on really good terms for a while, and by this time Ryan was about 7 months old. He was learning to sign words like "milk" and "more." Every time he did something new, I got super excited because this was all new for me and for him. It's almost like the first time a child says, "Dada." You get all happy and want to tell the world. I shared the news with DeVaughn and he said, "Now how in the fuck am I supposed to get excited about that?" It was like he took the air right out of my balloon. Talk about a joy stealer.

I knew DeVaughn was cruel, but wow, he was becoming a version of "the big bad wolf" right before my eyes. He wanted to control me, and he would get upset if I did something and didn't "ask for per-mission." For example, he'd say things like, "You didn't tell me you were hanging out with your so-called friends," if I happened to go out without calling. It was almost like I was his child, and I was being chastised. I decided to deal with him anyway, for whatever reason. To this day, I still can't figure it out. I thought that since he wasn't putting his hands on me it was alright. I wasn't aware of emotional or mental abuse at that time.

Dealing with DeVaughn made me lose focus on the main priority in my life, which was Ryan. Every time I had to be somewhere, I found myself calling him and letting him know where I was and what I was doing. Never mind the fact that I was an adult who paid her own bills. I felt that since he was there throughout my pregnancy I owed him something.

One day, I was out doing some shopping for Ryan's birthday when I ran into DeVaughn at the mall. I saw him before he saw me and he was with Felicia. I stepped into a store and called his cell phone. As I was hiding behind racks trying not to be seen, I saw him look at his phone, ignore the call and put it back in his pocket. Right then, my heart started to break. I couldn't even finish my shopping, because I didn't want to be seen, so I left the mall.

When I got home, I was playing with Ryan and DeVaughn just popped up. He asked me how my day was. I replied, "Cool, what did you do all day?"

He looked me right in my face and said, "I spent the day with my grandmother, because she's sick, why?"

"Stop lying, I saw you at the mall with Felicia."

I picked Ryan up and put him in his bedroom, because although he couldn't hear, he didn't need to see what was about to happen. When I got back to the living room and walked toward the couch, DeVaughn stood up and, from out of nowhere, backhanded me.

He said to me, "Bitch, don't be trying to see what the fuck I do. I'm yo man and if I said that's where I was, then don't question me."

As I laid on my couch crying, he kicked me and said, "I don't know who the fuck you think you are, you don't got no room to ask me a motherfucking thing. I'm through fucking with you, I'm gone."

Instead of letting him leave, I begged him to stay. I even apologized for being at the mall. I know it sounds crazy, huh? Dealing with cheating men, they always make you feel like their wrongdoings are your fault.

The moment I begged him to stay was the moment I told him his behavior was OK.

I went a few days without talking to him, but that never lasted long. He would call or buy me something and tell me he was sorry and vow to never do it again. I always got suckered back in. It went from the initial backhanded slap, to being choked until I passed out, having black eyes and even a hairline fracture in my nose. But every time he said, "I'm sorry," I let my guard down, only to be hurt worse as time went on.

By the time Ryan turned 1, the new Michael Jordan's were coming out. DeVaughn asked me to buy him a pair, and I told him I didn't have the money because I was planning my son's first birthday party. That didn't go over too well. He said to me, "I been with you since before that nigga came along and now you can't even buy me no shoes? Fuck you." Wow, can you imagine how I felt? But that didn't matter to him. I didn't buy the shoes, and I got an ass whooping for that too. It almost made me feel like I should have bought the shoes, then I wouldn't have gotten beat up.

Needless to say, I went to my son's first birthday party with a black eye and bruised ribs. I had to downplay it to my family and friends like nothing was going on. At the birthday party, I caught the attention of a nice looking guy. I knew he was watching me, but I didn't pay him any attention because of the amount of makeup on my face. I knew that if I was to get close enough to him, he'd see what everyone else had already noticed.

That didn't stop him from coming to me. He introduced himself as "Black." He had on a Coogi sweater, Polo jeans and some peanut butter-colored Timberland boots. Did I fail to mention how good he smelled? I told him my name was Isis, and that it was a pleasure to meet him. He asked me if I had a man, and I hesitated and said, "Yes, and no."

All through the conversation I kept my head down, so he wouldn't notice my face. For whatever reason, he wanted to look me in the eyes. He placed his hand on my chin and lifted my face up so we could see eye to eye. He noticed the makeup on my face and said, "You're a very gorgeous lady. Why are you wearing makeup?" I simply replied that I was using makeup to enhance my beauty. I told him I had to get back to the party, that if it was meant to be, we'd see each other again, and walked away.

Some time passed and things were just as bad as ever with DeVaughn. One day, we were at the mall together and I saw a familiar face. I wasn't sure why he was familiar to me, but when you see a face like his, it's one you can't get out of your mind. It was Black. He saw me, but didn't approach. He waited until the coast was clear then walked past and dropped a piece of paper by me. I bent down to pick it up, and the note read, "You're too good for Haze, and that explains the makeup. Call me." He left his number on the paper. I slid the note down in my boot so I wouldn't mistakenly leave it around the house.

When DeVaughn came back to where I was, I asked him how many nicknames he had. He looked confused, as if to say why are you asking such a random question, and he said, "I got a few, but I go by two."

I asked what they were, and he said, "D. Dave and Haze, why?"

I said, "When we first got together I heard people call you D. Dave, but I always called you DeVaughn. Then you mentioned the name Haze. Why do people call you that?"

He looked at me and said, "Don't you see my eyes?"

It still didn't make sense to me why some people called him one thing, and other people called him something else. I'll make it clear later.

As we were leaving the mall, he got a phone call and it was a girl on the other end. He said, "I'll be there in a minute." He then turned to me and said, "We gotta go."

I asked, "Was that Felicia?"

He grabbed my arm and pulled me close to him and said, "Don't worry about who calls my phone. I'm yo man. Don't ask me no questions."

The entire ride home I was quiet. He dropped me off and left. I didn't hear from him for about three days. During that time, I used the space between us to figure out what the difference was between DeVaughn, D. Dave and Haze. Although they were the same person, it didn't make sense to have so many aliases. I called Danielle, and asked her to call Tiffany and ask her if it was okay for me to call her. She did, and Tiffany said she didn't mind.

I spoke to Tiffany and what she said blew me away. Tiffany didn't hold back on sharing her past experiences with DeVaughn. She started off by saying, "If I had someone to kick real shit to me about these sorry-ass niggas, I would've kept walking past his sorry ass. I'm telling you straight up, he ain't shit. Don't get me wrong, that nigga can slang some dick, but don't get it twisted, he can swing them fists too. I don't want nobody to go through what I went through with his trifling ass. Let me tell you this, don't get sucked in by his sweet-talking bullshit, because like I said, it's bullshit."

As the conversation continued, she told me the difference between his three aliases, or what I called the "triple threat." "DeVaughn is who you meet when you first encounter him. He wants you to think that he's sweet, kind, and basically God's gift to all womankind. Then there's D. Dave. He's the dude that profiles, trying to be in with the real hood niggas. Don't get confused though, because he ain't 'bout that life that real niggas is about. He ain't sold nobody's drugs, and is too fucking scared to even pick up any type of gun. Finally, there's Haze, who is and will forever be a punk-ass nigga that hit on females. He'll fight a bitch before he even thinks twice about fighting a real goon."

The more she talked, the more it all began to make sense. All I could think to myself was, what have I gotten myself into? Furthermore, how could I get myself out of this madness?

When DeVaughn did finally reappear on the scene, I didn't ask him where he had been because I was almost at the point where I didn't care. I knew I deserved better, regardless of whatever situation I was in. Most importantly, Ryan didn't need to be nowhere near this maniac.

One day, I decided to just pick up the phone and call Black. He was about 6'2" and was as chocolate as they come. He wore his hair in a taper with waves that would make you seasick. His persona was very confident and he didn't care what people thought of him.

Black wasn't the hating type of dude, so to speak, but he did tell me something he thought I needed to know. He told me that DeVaughn had just become engaged to his "best friend." All this time, I never questioned his relationship with Michelle, because he said they were best friends. The fact that I now knew that it was more than friendship gave me a little more courage to leave him alone.

Mother's Day had just passed and DeVaughn called me and said he had a gift for me and wanted to bring it by. I had recently put Ryan to bed and gotten out of the shower. All I had on was my robe, and when he knocked on the door, I opened it. He carried a book bag with him, but I never paid it any attention.

He walked through the apartment, and asked, "Is anybody else here with you?"

"No, why?"

"Because I got something for you."

It wasn't unusual for him to bring me gifts, so I didn't think twice about it. He told me to take off my robe and sit in the chair. I did and he began to tie my hands behind my back and my feet to the legs of the chair. By then, I was getting freaked out about what he supposedly had for me.

"Who you fucking with?" he demanded.

"Nobody, why?"

"Don't lie to me, who you fucking?"

"I ain't fucking nobody. Why you asking me stupid-ass questions?"

"I know you fucking with somebody, so tell me who he is." Then he got down on his knees and began to pull my pubic hairs out one by one, still asking the same question.

"Who you fucking?"

"Nobody, now quit. That shit hurt."

He became irritated and punched me in my mouth, causing me to bite the left side of my jaw. He continued to pull out my pubic hairs.

He said, "Who is Black?"

"Just some dude I know. Why?"

"Oh, you fucking that nigga."

I began to cry, because he was causing me unbearable pain.

We argued about Black and he said, "If you want that nigga, be with him."

"Whatever, DeVaughn, don't get mad at me because you got engaged to Michelle. You can't control shit in two households."

That sent him over the edge. I guess he didn't think I knew about the engagement. After that, things got worse. He punched me in my face a few times, and told me I didn't know shit about no engagement.

Then he said, "What would happen if I just walk out and leave you here?"

"Ryan might wake up, and with the door being unlocked, he might go outside and get hit by a car."

Somehow, that convinced him to lock the door behind him as he left.

I was still sitting in the chair tied up. I managed to wiggle my hands free and then untie my feet. I double checked the lock and immediately called the police. When they arrived, I explained what just happened. They took pictures of my face, recorded my statement and told me they would attempt to find him. Then they gave me a case number and told me a detective would be contacting me.

The next day, I received a call from the detective's bureau requesting I come to the station to speak with the detective in person. Little did I know, the police had gone to DeVaughn's grandmother's house and tried to speak with him, but were unsuccessful. I told the detective that I wanted to think about pressing charges. He said, "I'm not telling you what to do, but don't wait too long. Dudes like this have tricks up their sleeves and you need to be cautious."

Later on that day, DeVaughn contacted me and gave me a very convincing story of how he wanted me to drop the charges so he could go play arena football in Minnesota. He said that if I dropped the charges, or didn't press them at all, he would leave me alone. Stupid me, I believed him and contacted my detective and told him I didn't wish to proceed. He strongly advised me not to ignore this, but ultimately he couldn't make the decision for me. Reluctantly, I let it go, only to find myself in a worse situation less than three weeks later.

On June 29, 2002, I invited Black over to chill and watch movies. It was getting late, about 3 a.m., but we were having fun just enjoying each other's company. Oddly, my phone rang. I answered it and lo and behold, it was DeVaughn on the other end.

"What you doing?"

"Nothing, don't call me no more." I hung up the phone.

A few seconds later, the phone rang again. I picked it up, and slammed it down. About 20 minutes later, there was a knock at the door.

"Who is it?" I asked.

No one answered, then the door flew open. There, a man stood in all black, a ski mask, yellow cleaning gloves and a 16" machete. I wasn't sure what to do. As he entered the apartment, he removed the mask. It was DeVaughn.

He took one look at Black and said, "If you wanna be alive tomorrow, then get the fuck out."

I swear I didn't think Black would leave, because he appeared to be a stand-up kind of nigga. Unfortunately, he bitched up and walked out. At that point, I was unsure of what was getting ready to take place. All I know is I was hoping Black made a call to the police and told them what was going on.

DeVaughn began yelling, saying, "What the fuck? You thought you was just gone hang up on me, and not have to pay for that bullshit? I know you know who the hell I am, bitch. I will kill you!"

All I could do was ask God to send me an angel to rescue me from death. Moments, which seemed like an eternity, passed, then my angel appeared. It was Ryan. He must have felt God wake him up and came looking for me. I know my prayer had to be answered, because being deaf, Ryan never wakes up through the night.

DeVaughn was so outraged that he didn't see Ryan walk up. The moment he saw Ryan, he immediately said to me, "You lucky Ryan woke, or I would've cut yo throat to the white meat." I grabbed Ryan and put him in my arms. Right then, I knew I would be alive to contact the police.

DeVaughn said to me, "I want some pussy."

"I'm on my period, I'm not fucking you."

"Bitch you ain't got no choice." Then he took his hand and slid it between my legs and said, "I don't feel no pad, I should smack you for lying."

"DeVaughn I'm wearing a tampon."

"Well, since you claim to be on yo period, then suck my dick."

"DeVaughn, I'm not sucking yo dick. I don't want to and if I don't do it right you gone get mad. I'm not sucking yo dick."

He grabbed Ryan out of my arms, and roughly sat him on the couch next to me. Then he yanked me by my arm and led me into my room. He pulled out his dick and forced my head to it.

"Suck my dick, bitch."

142

"I'm not sucking yo dick."

"Bitch, I said you ain't got no choice."

Then he slapped me in my face and forced his dick in my mouth. Ryan came to see about me, and out the corner of my eye I saw him standing in the doorway. I immediately pulled away, and DeVaughn got angry.

"What the fuck you stop for?"

"Ryan is here, DeVaughn."

He then dragged me into the bathroom, ordered me to take my panties off and remove my tampon. With that machete still in view, I did what he said. I didn't know what was getting ready to happen, so my best bet was to continue to go along with what I was being told. I removed the tampon and he snatched me by my arm and led me to the bed.

With Ryan still in the same room, DeVaughn grabbed Ryan and placed him on his chest as he laid on the bed. With Ryan facing him, DeVaughn pulled his penis out of his pants.

I told DeVaughn, "I'm not fucking you, so you need to get that thought out of your head."

He rose up off the bed, still with Ryan in his arms, picked up the machete and said, "You not doing what? Stay right here, I'll be back."

He put Ryan in the living room and came back to my bedroom. He then gripped me by my neck and bent me over my bed, forcing himself inside me. With tears in my eyes, trying not to let them fall, I thought to myself, if I had ever felt pain in my vaginal area, it was then. I had been through child birth, but nothing compares to a penis forcefully going into a semi-wet vagina.

At that moment, God sent my angel. Ryan came to save me. The fact that Ryan was standing there didn't stop DeVaughn. He began to thrust deeper and deeper, faster with every stroke. By this time I could feel my juice box getting dryer and dryer. It was starting to swell up with each push.

All during this trauma, all I could do was think about what Ryan must have been thinking, to see his mother being raped by someone he'd seen me with all of his life. I began to recite the 23rd Psalm. I felt my tears fall even faster, and despite the fact that I was wiping them, they didn't stop.

When I got to the part of the 23rd Psalm where it says, "Yea thou I walk through the valley of the shadow of death, I will fear no evil, for thou art with me," I was interrupted by DeVaughn saying, "I'm coming." He pulled out, turned me around and attempted to ejaculate his semen on me. Fortunately, it fell on the floor. He pulled up his pants, and said, "Now that should be reason enough for you to call the police."

I took Ryan and locked us in the bathroom. As I was holding him, I couldn't do anything but thank God for sending me Ryan. Although he witnessed what he did, it could've been a lot worse. He could've seen me killed.

I waited in the bathroom until I heard nothing at all. I opened the door to look out into my apartment and saw that the door was left open, with the frame damaged from being kicked in. All this took place while my door was open and no one bothered to come and see what was going on.

I called the police, and they responded in minutes. As luck would have it, it was the exact same officers who were at my house three weeks earlier. When the female officer looked at me, her first words were, "What did he do, and where is he now?" I gave my report, and she said she would find him, and for me not to worry.

About two hours later, she contacted me and told me they had him in custody. Praise God. It was at that moment I realized why he was called the beast with the hazel eyes. If only I had heeded the signs, I wouldn't have gone through this. But it was too late to sing my shoulda, coulda, woulda's.

Over the next six months, we were in and out of court. Finally, the trial came, and I had to relive that experience all over again. It took the jury a little over four hours to find him guilty on the four counts he was being charged with. Two counts of criminal sexual conduct (orally & vaginally), home invasion and felonious assault. That was a relief for me.

A month later we were back for the sentencing. The judge gave him 12-15 years, but he'd be eligible for parole in six.

As for Ryan and me, now that that chapter was closed, I felt I could start our life over. And that's exactly what I did.

Dear Isis,

I can't judge you for making mistakes, because we all do. My prayer is that you learn from this. Although it ended the way it did, it could've been a lot worse. Be wise in your decision making, man choosing, and subliminal signs that may be there. My advice to you is to get in your Bible and develop a relationship with God, because He's the only One who will save you in your time of need. I love you, and I hope you learned a valuable lesson. Remember, what you went through was definitely not for you. It happened so you can tell someone else that they can make it out and it doesn't have to end like your story ended. Share your story and help another young lady. I love you.

NOTES

/

Lisa Stefanski

Lisa Stefanski is the author of the memoir *No Longer Hidden, No Longer Ashamed*. She was born and raised in Essexville, Michigan. She has a degree in Special Education and spent 18 years working in the mental health field, where she actively advocated for people with developmental disabilities.

In 2007, she moved to Flint, Michigan where she currently resides with her partner and their two dogs. She has made it a lifelong goal to help raise awareness to the effects of childhood sexual abuse.

THE COURAGE TO FORGIVE
Lisa Stefanski

Some people might think that hitting rock bottom for me was when I attempted to take my life. It wasn't. I didn't really want to die, but I did not know how to live with the pain I was carrying around inside.

I grew up in a middle class family in a small town with two brothers and a sister. I was happy, innocent and my life was perfect.

That perfect life ended around the age of 5. That is when my neighbor started to sexually abuse me. My happiness was taken away, tainting my world with darkness and evil.

The abuse continued for several years.

Around the age of 7, I decided to share the secret with my mom. I can't describe the fear that I was feeling. I am sure it was very similar to a person with arachnophobia having to hold a spider. I was carrying around so much shame that I did not know how to share it.

There I sat, alone with my mom in the kitchen, paralyzed. I was trying to summon my inner strength to tell my mom what the neighbor was doing to me. I was only 7 years old and already I was being controlled by my "secret." After several minutes, I was finally able to find the courage to tell my mom that the neighbor touched me "down there."

I remember the look on her face — that blank stare. She stood there in the hallway, staring at me. She

151

did not say a word, she just stared. We never — even until this day — talked about it again. Her reaction to me was worse than the abuse itself.

I wish someone would have told me then that this wasn't my fault, because as a child, I internalized everything, from the abuse itself to how much it upset my mom. From my mom's reaction, I concluded I never should have told.

These experiences in my childhood took away much more than my innocence; they broke me. They broke every part of me. As a result, I learned to keep everything bottled up inside.

By the age of 13, I was running away from home, shoplifting, stealing cars, fighting, and having sex with people just because they asked. I had so much unresolved pain inside, I started cutting myself. I did not know any other way to relieve the pain. Secretly, I was hoping someone would notice and help fix me. At that point in my life I wasn't sure what was wrong. I was labeled the "problem child," and was told that I acted out because I "wanted attention."

No one knew the pain I was holding inside, including me. No one took the time to explain to me that what happened to me as a child was wrong and not my fault. What I came to realize though, was that you can't fix something unless you know why it's broken. Until that point I had no idea. So I embraced the "problem child" role and that became my identity. Let me tell you, if they were to hand out medals for problem children — I was winning the gold!

During this time, my parents had enough of my acting out and decided to put me in therapy. My entire family went to the first appointment together. My mom and dad sat in that room and talked about me to this lady that I didn't even know. They told her how much trouble I was in (they had not seen anything yet).

Then I remember the therapist asking if I had been sexually abused. I'll never forget my body's reaction. My face became flushed, my muscles stiffened, and my body temperature started to rise. I was getting pissed. Then I heard mom say, "No."

Mom and the therapist agreed the neighbors were just kids and determined that I had not been sexually abused. As a 5-year-old, why don't you have a teenager ask you to kiss his hard penis and tell me what you think.

My family never talked about any problems. We were always taught to just be quiet and pretend that everything was okay. As a result, I internalized everything. Finally, the pain became too great and I turned to anything that would help me numb it.

I was lost and there was no finding me.

Around the same age, I also started drinking, experiencing my first blackout shortly after. Before that, I had taken everything life threw at me and swallowed it. I never let anyone know the pain I was holding inside.

I started to experiment with drugs too. I took speeders mostly, but I tried LSD and marijuana as well. But nothing that I had done prepared me for what would eventually happen. In my early 20s I was introduced to cocaine. Shortly after, my world came crashing down.

I can recall the night like it was yesterday. I was hanging out at the bar with some friends. I remember going into the bathroom and seeing that first line of cocaine on the back of the toilet.

There are so many slogans and campaigns out there that state, "Just say NO." I wish I would have listened.

By that time in my life, I was trying to forget everything about myself. I wanted to erase all the pain I was carrying around. I did everything I could not to feel it. Using cocaine seemed like the perfect opportunity to help me forget — it wasn't. It caused me to create many more demons that I still fight with every day.

To me, there is a big difference in acknowledging the pain that someone else caused you, and the pain that you caused yourself.

I remember staring at that line of cocaine. I felt afraid and excited at the same time. With the straw from a mixed drink, I began the habit that almost destroyed me. The euphoria I felt doing that first line was overwhelming. It was indescribable. It would not be long until I was in its full grip.

It started with that simple line of coke and quickly spiraled out of control. Shortly after I started using cocaine, it was the only thing that helped me forget the pain. I started out using it only on the weekends. When I could not find any, I would snort other things — anything that I could get my hands on

— like Ritalin. I am sure I snorted a few other things too, I just don't remember.

Soon, cocaine was the only thing I looked for.

One winter night, we had snorted all we had and I still wanted more. The dealer was not answering his phone, so someone I was with at the time suggested we get some crack. She said she had used it before and tried to describe it to me — I was all for it.

I guess I should have looked around and realized what crack would lead me to. We were at my friend's house; it was rented. She had no furniture in the living room. The TV was sitting on the floor and had a coat hanger attached to help with reception. Her bed was just a mattress on the floor in a bedroom. She had no cooking utensils. The only food in her house was in dented cans. She did not own a can opener and tried to open them, without success, with other things.

I should have considered my surroundings and seen the outcome, but I did not. I was so consumed with forgetting my pain that I drove us to the crack house. When we went inside, it was one of the darkest places I have ever been to. There were rooms with sheets over the door frames. I don't even want to imagine what was going on behind those sheets.

We purchased the crack and went back to my friend's house. She put it in the pipe for me and explained how to inhale. I put the pipe to my mouth and she lit it. I inhaled, and knew by the end of the night that my life as I knew it was over.

With cocaine, I usually only used it on the weekends. With crack, I wanted it all the time. I would go to work just so I had money to satisfy my habit. I spent all of my money on it. I started out with two savings accounts. One was for my daily living and the other was money that I was saving to buy a house. I told myself as long as I had the secondary account, I did not have a problem. That was a lie, a lie that I realized too late.

I emptied my primary savings account in a few months. Then I started on my secondary account. I could not stop, I wanted more and more. When my secondary account was gone, I started with the credit cards. I would do cash advances. I would buy the dealer jewelry and shoes in exchange for crack. When the credit cards were maxed out, I sold my belongings. I even went as far as signing over the title for my Tracker until I could get more cash.

It wasn't until I had spent all my money, maxed out my credit cards and sold my belongings that I truly knew what rock bottom was, because I still wanted to get high. I hurt so bad inside that I did not want to stop. So with nothing left, I sold the only thing I had.

I sold myself.

Everyone has boundaries they set for themselves. They have things that they say they will never do. This was one of mine. No matter how much pain the dealer showed me, nothing could compare to the agony I was causing myself. I became my own worst enemy. Now I was the one who was causing the pain, all because I could not leave this little white rock alone.

With time, most pain starts to fade or at least lose its intensity. I woke up every day waiting for that to happen. I waited for the pain to go away, but it didn't. Day after day, what happened in that hotel room dominated my thoughts. It was relentless, demoralizing pain. Even today, I get goose bumps thinking about it.

How do you justify pain you cause yourself?

How?

I still don't have an answer to that.

When I finally had enough — because I could not quit crack — I tried to take my own life. That night was one of the darkest nights of my life. I had caused myself so much mental pain and anguish. The things I did played over and over in my mind. I did not know how to make it stop. I hated my world; I hated me!

It was nighttime and I was drunk. I drove myself to the local 24-hour store. I had to urinate on the way, but did not want to pull over to relieve myself, so I peed on myself while I was driving. I walked into the store smelling of urine and bought several bottles of sleeping pills and a few cans of beer. I drove myself someplace where I thought no one would find me. I started to take those sleeping pills, one after another. I continued taking them, prepared to never wake up again. I wanted to end all the pain. One by one I swallowed them. I finished the first bottle and started on the second, pill after pill, becoming more tired with each passing minute, until finally, I fell asleep.

By the grace of God, my life did not end that night.

I woke up in the inpatient mental health ward at the hospital. Before that day, I had been there three or four times. One of the first people I saw was my little sister. She said to me, "How could you be so selfish?" My little sister is my best friend. She means the world to me. But even she did not understand what was going on, because I hid the majority of my life from everyone. I only let them see what I wanted them to see.

Hiding everything created even more shame for me. By hiding, I gave my demons power. I was living my life and doing things that were so embarrassing that I did not want to admit to them.

"How could you be so selfish?" Those words rang in my head and made me do a lot of thinking. Have you ever felt so alone that even you did not know yourself? That was where I was in life. I had no idea who I was. Everything in my life wasn't bad. There were some parts that were, but everything wasn't. Killing myself would take away all the good things I had too.

It was then that I decided I did not want to die, but I did not know how to live with the pain that I caused myself. I was my worst enemy and I was doing everything I said I would never do. I had crossed all of my boundaries and broken all of my morals and now I had to start picking up the pieces and learn to live again.

I started out by trying to stop using drugs. That was something that took a little work, but I was determined. I was not successful right away, but eventually my cravings lessened. I started going to therapy again. I had been in therapy throughout my life, but was never successful. I could not share the things that I found too painful to talk about. I was hoping that if I ignored my pain long enough it would go away. It didn't. It was only when I started to take down the wall that I had been building for over 25 years that I actually started to heal.

I had to admit to a lot of things that I am very ashamed of. There were things that not only hurt me, but hurt others as well. Some parts I could only admit to when I was ready. I had to admit to something that happened to me as a child. I spent over 25 years holding inside that I was sexually abused. This was almost three-quarters of my life. Some people knew that things happened to me, but no one knew the extent.

Being sexually abused as a child broke that little girl inside of me. It took away her innocence, her self-worth and her self-esteem. For a long time, I blamed her for what happened. I blamed her because I was judging her through the eyes of an adult. I was judging her based on the knowledge I had as an adult, but in reality she was just a little girl who was hurt.

As I continued in therapy, I started to understand myself. I began to understand my actions and the reasons behind them. This was a huge breakthrough for me, because as I began to understand myself, I also learned to forgive myself. As a child, someone hurt me; they broke me and no one helped me understand or put myself back together. So for over 25 years, I walked the earth lost and hurt.

If I could go back in time, there are so many things that I would do differently. If I could find that little girl that I once was, I would hold her and tell her everything will be alright. I would protect her and cherish her like all children should be. I would encourage her to talk about her pain. She was not the one who caused it, but she was the one living with it.

Life is not always fair. Everyone has their own unique set of circumstances. Everyone deals with their own pain. This is part of what makes us human. No one likes to talk about the bad things in life. They are not pleasant. Sometimes they are very uncomfortable. At times they are shameful. They may even hurt. Just because they are unpleasant though, does not mean they did not happen.

I wish I could have recognized this back then. For me, holding in all of my pain and hurt led me to a very dark place. I wish years ago, someone would have taught me how to speak up for myself.

We all make mistakes in life and do things that we regret. We may say something that hurts someone else or do something that hurts ourselves.

What do you do when you cause yourself so much pain that you no longer want to live? You try to understand why you did it and learn to forgive.

That night in that hotel room was the lowest point in my life. Regardless of what happened inside that room, no one hurt me more than I did. Imagine sinking so low that you betray yourself. You hurt yourself more than anyone else ever could.

I will never be able to apologize enough to myself. The fact remains that I cannot go back and change what happened and what I did. What I can do though, is love and protect myself today.

Don't beat yourself up for things that have happened in your past. You can no longer control it or change it. It's over. Learn to embrace it and accept it. Don't run from it. It took every ounce of courage that I could find to acknowledge my past. But once I did, I started to beat the demons that were ruling my world.

Today I wake up each morning with a smile on my face and tell the world that today is going to be the best day of my life.

Remember, the decisions you make today create the memories you will have tomorrow. Make them good ones!

NOTES

Danielle E. Ward

Danielle E. Ward is the author of *Warning Signs: What every woman should know — A dating guide*. Outside of writing, Ms. Ward works as a freelance sign language interpreter and editor.

Danielle's education includes a Bachelor of Science in Chemistry from Hampton University, a Master of Arts in Interpretation from Gallaudet University, a certificate in Radio Broadcasting from the Columbia School of Broadcasting and a certificate from The Word and the Spirit Bible Training Center.

Ms. Ward is an avid volunteer and enjoys reading, sports, board games and traveling. She resides in Flint, Michigan with her son.

Learn more about Danielle E. Ward at www.danielleward.me.

IT'S JUST HAIR, RIGHT?
Danielle E. Ward

Here we go again, I sighed. I guess this is what it comes down to.

You see, I was ending a 30+ year love affair — with my hair. After seven years of locs, I was headed to the barbershop the next day to cut my hair down to a bald fade.

As I watched a movie with my son, I cut off loc after loc, and unceremoniously threw each one in the trash.

Why keep a reminder of what obviously isn't supposed to be? I thought. Enough with the pomp and circumstance. I mean, it's just hair, right?

Wrong.

It was April 5, 2011. This would mark the day I officially divorced my hair. Let me take you back to where it all began.

When I was a little girl, my mom always braided my hair. I had cornrows, French braids, ribbons, beads and bangs. She made sure I looked my best.

I remember second grade vividly. It was the year of the Jheri curl, and I wanted one. My mother agreed, and I was thrilled to leave the braids behind and transition to a free-flowing hairstyle. This was the ticket to having my hair loose and long and being able to try new styles like my white friends and the black ones with perms.

By this point in my life, I was well indoctrinated in the mindset that long, flowing hair was the prettiest. I don't recall hearing it from my parents, but the voice of two was largely overshadowed by the commercials and dolls I played with.

Needless to say, I was crushed, when shortly after getting my coveted Jheri curl, my hair started to fall out. This was my first experience with chemicals in my hair, and my body rejected them.

Second grade is a time when kids want to assimilate — everyone wants glasses if their best friend just got them; if the cute boy has braces, the girls fawning after him have to have braces too.

Well, it was no different with hair. You can imagine how devastated I was when I realized I was down to two choices — wear a wig until my hair grew back or cut it off and start from scratch. I wasn't about to wear a wig and risk being teased, or worse, having it yanked off by that day's prankster. No ma'am. So I decided to cut it off.

There's a song titled, "The First Cut Is The Deepest," sung by Sheryl Crow. Although she's not singing about hair, that title aptly describes how I felt, sitting in the beautician's chair watching my hair fall in clumps to the floor. I don't remember if I cried or not. Probably, but I had to develop a thick skin pretty quickly. I had to go to school the next day. Anyone who's been among the least popular knows how cruel kids (and adults) can be, so I needed a certain resolve to survive the next few months looking like a little boy until my hair grew back.

Eventually, my hair did begin to grow back. Instead of chemicals, we opted for the press 'n curl. As many of us know, press 'n curl is cute — until you hit the heat, water, or sweat it out. It just wasn't practical for the tomboy I was.

By fourth grade, my mom found someone to put braid extensions in my hair. It was nice having lots of options in styling my hair. Sitting for hours, sometimes up to eight hours, wasn't always fun, but once she was done, I loved it. I experimented with all sorts of styles, colors and lengths. Every three months, I was able to reinvent myself.

Middle school proved to be quite impactful, yet another test of my inner strength.

I remember one evening after track practice someone telling me that a guy in eighth grade had been calling me 'The Predator,' referring to a recent movie release. I had never watched the movie, but once I saw what I was being compared to, I couldn't believe someone would be so mean. This creature was gruesome to look at, though I believe I was only being compared to it because it had long locks of hair that resembled my extensions.

It was bad enough I was skinny and small. To realize I was the butt of a joke over something I was finally feeling good about let me know I'd never fit in completely, no matter what my hair looked like.

Then came eighth grade …

My mom and I thought that perhaps the Jheri curl from second grade was too strong for my scalp. We assumed that a "kiddie" perm, or a perm supposedly less harsh than a regular perm, would be better for my sensitive scalp.

Let me fast forward to present day for a moment. To aid in my preparation for this piece, a friend suggested I watch the movie *Good Hair* starring Chris Rock. It was actually more of a documentary than a movie, as it sought to understand black women's views on hair.

There was one clip where the topic of perms came up. Rock interviewed women and girls about the age they were when they got their first perm and why. Most mentioned getting a perm because they felt it made their hair more manageable. Some girls had perms as young as three years old.

What struck me during this segment was the experiment Rock did with a chemist. There were several bins containing Coke cans submerged in perm chemicals. After certain times had elapsed, the cans were removed and the results were noted. The purpose was to demonstrate the effects of a "kiddie" perm on the cans, which represented a person's scalp. One can was almost completely melted by the time it was removed from the solution containing sodium hydroxide, the main ingredient in lye perms.[1] This is the same chemical found in many industrial solvents and cleaners, such as floor-stripping products, cements, brick cleaners, etc. It's even used to clear drains and polish metal.[2]

This is what I was putting in my hair? This is what so many young girls' tender little scalps were being subjected to?

Interviewees even commented on the burn of the chemicals and how they would grin and bear it a while longer because it meant their hair would be that much straighter.[3] A worthy sacrifice, right? I sure thought so.

Research has shown that sodium hydroxide is poisonous, through inhalation, touch and ingestion. Side effects listed included breathing difficulty, lung inflammation, throat swelling, skin burns and irritation and necrosis, or holes in the skin or underlying tissues.[4]

If you have been in a beauty salon, you know how many people are getting perms simultaneously and inhaling this stuff every six weeks, for hours at a time, without proper ventilation. Let's not forget to mention the stylists who are applying the perms, many of whom wear thin latex gloves.

This leads me to question, if it's caustic enough for them to wear gloves to protect their skin, why are they smearing this dangerous chemical directly onto the scalp of their clients?

Back to eighth grade. The perm took, but just like before, it started to fall out after a short while. If I thought it was hard the first time, it was even more difficult the second time around. Yes, I had done this before, so being 'baldheaded,' as I was often called, shouldn't have been a big deal. In second grade, maybe not, but eighth grade? Hormones are raging and guys and girls are actually looking at each other and not saying, "Eww."

Being baldheaded was definitely not going to help my cause. On top of that, I was going to high school the next year — I couldn't go with no hair.

I had no choice except to cut it. To try and be fashionable with it and make the transition easier for me, my mom glued rhinestones in a 'V' pattern along my hairline. I will never forget how self-conscious I felt that first day back at school. I was sitting in the front of the room and could practically feel the eyes and whispers of my classmates behind me as they got a glimpse of my new 'do.

Despite the looks, the short 'fro remained and I ended up keeping it that way for a little while. Eventually, I ended up back in braid extensions until it was time for senior pictures.

I was determined to wear my hair — my own hair — down for senior pictures. I was becoming tired of being stuck in braids and felt my last high school photos should be special. Because my hair wasn't very voluminous, my beautician added a hair piece to increase the body. I wasn't too comfortable with the idea of a weave, but I tried it and my pictures came out great. Nevertheless, I haven't worn a weave since that day.

Speaking of weaves, that movie *Good Hair* broached the topic. I almost choked on my popcorn as I listened to these women go on and on about how much they spent on weaves. One woman admitted easily spending as much as $18,000 a year on hair alone[5] — not including the styling of said hair, just the hair itself. Unbe"weave"able! You could buy a car with that kind of money or put a down payment on a house!

This information shocked and saddened me, to know all that hard-earned money was going toward the purchase of another human's hair, all to present a certain image and make a statement. What made the whole situation worse was when Chris Rock traveled to India to see the source of this human hair obsession.

Men and women alike were shaving their heads as, they believed, a sacrifice to God, while those in power were shipping it by the truckload to places like the U.S. Even babies were not exempt from this practice.[6] I was disgusted to see this misrepresentation as the country raked in money from the sale of these people's hair.

Let me get off my soapbox and get back to my story. High school ended, and I headed off to college. I was still wearing extensions, but faced a slight dilemma. Who was going to do my hair? I never learned how to do it myself, and didn't know people in the area. Thankfully, family came to my aid. I had a relative not too far away who could maintain my hair for me.

These appointments continued until the end of sophomore year. I had earned a summer internship to Dar es Salaam, Tanzania, to perform chemistry research. I was beyond excited, and of course back to the eternal question, "Who's gonna do my hair?"

Not wanting the stress, I made a decision — did you catch that? I made the choice — to cut my hair.

By this time, my natural hair was just about grazing my shoulders. I sat down and told the barber I wanted it all off. When he finished cutting and I looked in the mirror, I told him to cut it some more. The next time I saw my reflection, a big smile appeared. It was perfect.

This time the length of my hair didn't bother me. I was free, no longer tied to the whims of my scalp. I was in control of my hair for the first time in my life, ever. It was one of the best decisions I have made.

Those three and a half months I spent in Tanzania were fabulous. There was no worry about my hair. I was able to come and go with a carefree spirit I'd never experienced before. Interestingly enough, in Dar es Salaam, the girls are forced to wear a short 'fro until they graduate from high school. This is to avoid unnecessary distractions and focus on learning. After graduation, they can style their hair as they please. Naturally, I was questioned about my desire to wear my hair short when I could've worn any style I wanted.

I don't know if it was my confidence or hairstyle — maybe a bit of both — but men were finding me attractive and approaching me with short hair this time. I had a bald fade before a lot of women were wearing them, so maybe there was a certain mystique that made men want to know more about me. I don't know, but it was definitely nice to be noticed.

Of course having little to no hair had its downside as well. On more than one occasion I was assumed to be a lesbian, and a couple of times I was mistaken for a cancer patient.

During the early years of having a short haircut, I experimented with hair dye. I didn't want to be a 'Plain Jane,' and I wanted to venture out and be daring. No limits, right? Plus I was in college. What better time to try something new?

The first time I tried dyeing my own hair, I used a color combination recommended by a friend. It was a lovely duet of Crème Soda and Spiced Cognac, not too much, but enough to notice my hair was a different color.

My hair didn't turn out too bad, but I did notice certain sections of my hair were a bit darker than others in places. Odd, but I chalked it up to inexperience.

When I went to the barbershop to cut it, I had a pretty embarrassing episode. My barber was cutting my hair down to help make the color difference less noticeable. As he cut, in addition to my hair dropping to the floor, all these orange-ish flakes were falling around me like colored snow.

I didn't know what was going on. I didn't have dandruff, and I used hair products regularly to keep my scalp moisturized. He looked at me incredulously and asked, "What did you do to your hair?" After I explained, he got a white towel — not a colored towel to camouflage my mess — and proceeded to wipe my head down to get rid of as many flakes as he could. I eventually left with a nice cut, but not without leaving a piece of my dignity behind.

When I went to Albuquerque, N.M., the following summer, I tried to amp things up a bit and dyed my hair blonde. Boy was I in for a big surprise. When my hair was finished, I looked in the mirror and saw a calico cat staring back at me! Parts of my hair were bright blonde, and other areas were a darker blonde. I had to cut my hair almost bald before I was comfortable leaving the house. After the cut, I loved how it looked. The sun would hit it at just the right angle to make it shimmer. Between the two colors, blonde was definitely my favorite.

Since I liked blonde so much, I decided to try it again when I came home. I made an appointment with my beautician, and wouldn't you know it, she had the same problem I did. Evidently, it wasn't about reading directions. It was about knowing how my hair reacted to the dye. For some reason, different parts didn't take the same. Even with her leaving the dye on for more time in some places and less in others in an attempt to balance out the color, the results were the same. This occurred in 1999, and was the last time I dyed or put any other chemicals in my hair.

During my undergrad years, I was mostly approached by men during my summer internships. There weren't too many men comfortable with my short hair at my college. Long hair, real or fake, still reigned supreme at that time. It was their loss. I'm sure having a fade saved me from potential relationship drama and distractions, so I won't complain.

While my college peers were still emerging from the stereotypes of what beautiful looked like, I was embraced when I arrived in D.C. Compared to undergrad, I would say graduate school was the time I felt the most attractive with short hair. I was complimented more often and approached by not only black men, but white men too. My hair did not cause these men to look away and write me off as someone they'd never date. My hair was a part of what made me beautiful and drew them to me in an attempt to get to know me better.

I knew deep down that I was pretty no matter what my hair looked like — and my short hair was becoming. I wouldn't have worn it that way otherwise. Plus, my mother, known for her inability to mince words, would have told me. However, after all of my hair debacles over the years, and the societal misconceptions about true beauty, it was nice to be affirmed.

I met my husband while finishing up my second year of grad school. I still had a low cut when we met and eventually married. Ironically, he told me he actually preferred women with long hair, and that I was the first person he'd dated with barely any. I did have more hair than he did, since he was bald, so maybe that helped. I must admit that after he told me his preference, I intentionally did not grow my hair out. I had no immediate plans to do so anyway, but I wanted to be sure I was being accepted as I was, not accepted with plans to change me into someone else. To his credit, my husband never once asked me to grow it.

By 2004, I was ready to try something new. I had just given birth to a son and returned to Michigan. Wanting to remain natural and wear only my own hair, I decided to try dreadlocks.

I began my loc journey with Sisterlocks, a process of locking the hair in a way that had immediate permanence, compared with the traditional locking method of palm rolling that could take locs several months to fully form. With Sisterlocks, I would have the freedom to do things like wash my hair and swim right away, activities I wouldn't be able to do if my hair was palm-rolled.

After finding a local loctitian, my locs began with only about an inch and a half of hair. That's a pretty short length to start with, but my loctitian was confident she could make it work.

As my locs were growing, my hair went through many phases. Sometimes, I would wrap my head in a scarf and go to work. I did this when my hair needed to be retightened, when it was in a phase I wasn't sure how to handle or if I simply wanted to wrap my hair.

One of my coworkers started to take notice and would ask, "What are you doing to your hair? You always wrap it right before you do something different."

I guess I wasn't on my journey alone — people were paying attention. That was a bit uncomfortable, especially since this process was a first for me. I was learning as I went, not always sure what my hair would look like when I gazed in the mirror each day. I had the eyes of all of my coworkers on me as I navigated my way through this experience. It had to be done, but there were days when I wished I could've cocooned myself and emerged with nice, long locs.

I tried to make sure I followed my loctitian's instructions on hair care. Here's an example of one of our first, and only, conversations.

Me: Now you know I have never taken care of my own hair before. I have only had braids or a fade. What should I put on it?

Her: You can put whatever you want on your scalp. I use (whatever she named), but buy whatever works for you. Just keep your scalp and hair moisturized. You should use Crème of Nature in the orange bottle to wash and condition.

Me: Okay, should I tie my locs up at night?

Her: If you want. It's really up to you.

You can clearly see how this could've been a struggle for me. For someone who has never taken care of her own hair to be given complete flexibility with no definitive instructions was a recipe for disaster.

Despite the lack of guidance, things were progressing nicely. It didn't take long for my locs to grow and look really good. I was so excited. Not only was my hair longer than it had ever been, it was all mine. Plus, I could try new styles whenever I wanted. I thought about dyeing it, but with my hair doing so well, I didn't want to risk adding unnecessary chemicals.

Then it happened. One day, I noticed a bald spot in the crown of my head. It was about the size of a dime. My loctitian didn't know what it was or what to do with it, so she left it alone and worked around it. She thought perhaps my scalp was just dry, so I tried to do a better job of keeping it moisturized. My efforts were in vain. The spot didn't go away; it got bigger.

I was frustrated. I finally had some hair to work with, and now I was having problems, again. Talk about a letdown. I wasn't ready to give up the fight yet, so I continued to see my loctitian. After several missed appointments and poor excuses, I left her and decided I'd figure out how to do my hair myself.

I tried doing my own locs, but had neither the know-how, patience nor desire to do it. I opted to try traditional locs this time, because while Sisterlocks were more convenient in terms of my hair locking immediately, there were more loctitians using the traditional method. I didn't want to get stuck again with no one around to lock my hair.

I found a loctitian from someone I knew and she seemed very knowledgeable about hair. Upon looking at mine, she commented on how dry my scalp was, and proceeded to rescue my scalp with a special shampoo and conditioner, then gave me recommendations on home hair care. This loctitian even started working on my bald spot, trying to stimulate growth in that area.

Initially, I was feeling encouraged. I thought things would begin to improve and I would see some growth. My hair did start looking healthier, but that didn't come without a cost.

"Greasy" is the best word I can think of to describe my hair. Everything my hair touched had oil spots on it. For a minute, I felt like I was back in the days of the Jheri curl, when people would joke about Jheri curl "juice" being everywhere. Not only was my hair greasy, but because it was so heavy from product, I could no longer style it. All my locs did was hang there. Gone were the days of light, curly and carefree. I was a greasy, heavy mess. I had hair though, so it still counted for something, I guess.

After one too many flake-outs by my stylist, and the bald spot not growing in, I left the professional world of styling and transitioned back to Sisterlocks, with the help of my mom.

I must pause and give kudos to my mom. No matter what my hair was doing, she was right alongside me, learning as she went. The majority of my hairstyles were a result of what she taught herself. You couldn't tell her work from a professional's. I really appreciate her desire to make sure I was always presentable and confident in my appearance.

During this time, I visited a few dermatologists, hoping to get to the root of my scalp issue. Not only was my hair not growing properly, but I was experiencing tenderness in certain places on my scalp. It was as if my nerve endings were standing on alert and every touch would send shocks of pain through my scalp. There weren't too many dermatologists who were familiar with black people's hair in my area, but I hoped for the best.

The first two didn't have much to say about the bald spot, except that maybe my hair was being pulled too tight and my scalp couldn't handle it. The second doctor suggested that the scalp tenderness might have resulted from changes in estrogen levels in my body, sometimes worsening during my menstrual cycle. I had developed a habit of pulling out my hair with tweezers until I could locate the hair that was giving me the trouble. Many times I ended up with bald patches and would have to cover them up. This doctor told me as long as pulling the hair out helped, he saw no reason not to.

The third and final dermatologist I saw had the idea of performing a biopsy to see exactly how my scalp was behaving under the surface. He assured me my hair would grow back in the place where the biopsy occurred. It sounded like a good idea to me.

Because of his guarantee, instead of picking an inconspicuous place, I told him to take a sample from the exact spot where I was having the most trouble. It made sense to me to go right to the source.

The biopsy revealed that I had a condition known as *alopecia areata*, which basically means hair loss. Lots of people were running around saying they had *alopecia*, so I wasn't impressed yet.

The doctor then told me that under my scalp, scar tissue had formed. As a result, the scar tissue was blocking the flow of oxygen to the blood, which in turn was preventing hair growth. He also explained that this scar tissue could've been formed from scratching or brushing too hard, braiding or locking too tight, or anything else that would cause my scalp to be irritated and protect itself with a scar. He told me stress might be a factor in the hair not growing back. As for pulling out my hair, the doctor cautioned me against it, informing me that it wasn't good for my scalp to undergo that type of trauma.

Recent research according to the National Alopecia Areata Foundation shows this type of hair loss is classified as an autoimmune skin disease that affects the scalp and other parts of the body where hair grows. The initial symptoms are what I experienced, "one or more small, round smooth patches on the scalp." Apparently, *alopecia areata* has been diagnosed in about 2 percent of the world, with more than 6.5 million of those people residing in the U.S. The Foundation research supports that the disease occurs in cycles and a pattern can't be predicted — hair loss and growth can occur at any time — it's completely individual.[7]

As for solutions, I now know that the FDA hasn't approved any kind of treatment for *alopecia areata*. However, many doctors try to reverse symptoms with such things as cortisone injections, topical creams and ointments, pills and immuno-therapy.[8]

Not having this knowledge at the time and seeing the results of another woman who had cortisone injections, I chose this course of treatment for myself.

The doctor explained that the purpose of the injections was to break down the built-up scar tissue so oxygen could get to the blood and stimulate hair growth — basically reverse the process. I was supposed to notice hair growth after six visits. If I didn't, the damage was done, and there wasn't much more they could do.

Each injection consisted of about four shots in each affected area of my scalp. It was so painful that I asked the nurse if she had ever had that done to her head. Surprisingly, she said they had to experience it to know what it would feel like with patients. It still hurt. And to make matters worse, the most I ever got was a bit of fuzz in that area. The biopsy site never did grow hair again. You can still see the scar from the incision. Just another battle wound as far as I'm concerned.

Meanwhile, I still had my locs and was essentially hiding behind my hair. The freedom I initially experienced was no longer there. I felt confined and discouraged because even though I had hair — my own hair — that was past my shoulders, all I could do was let it hang there.

If I styled it, the bald spot might show, and I definitely didn't want that. I was even starting to lose locs because of the thinning, so I was trying to cover that up as well. It was becoming too much.

I tried holding on a little while longer, in hopes that maybe the injections just needed more time to work. When it became painfully obvious that this wasn't the case, I made the decision to cut it off and be done. It wasn't a difficult choice, but it was disappointing. I had worn locs for seven years and I felt like I was back at square one — making decisions based on what my scalp dictated.

This feeling made me think back to a song by India.Arie, "I Am Not My Hair." I was driving down the street listening to the radio when I first heard it. You could have knocked me over with a feather — she was practically telling my hair's life story. Outside of a timeline a few years off and some of the hairstyles in different order, our experiences mirrored each other.

Now, I am not an impulse buyer by any means, but I tell you what — I went and bought that single so fast you'd have thought it was the last one on the shelf and had a prize inside.

"I Am Not My Hair" became my anthem. I'd push in my CD, press repeat and drive, singing at the top of my voice. This song represented every stage my hair had undergone. I had never felt completely alone in my journey, but to find someone who related so well was uncanny.

Ultimately, like her refrain states, "I went on and did what I had to do."[9] That day in the barber's chair was bittersweet. On one hand, I was again following my hair's lead. On the other hand, I wasn't navigating unchartered waters. I had had short hair before and liked how it looked.

In an effort to maintain some sort of control, I made a vow that since I was cutting it off again, I was eventually going to try the bald look. I mean, why not go all the way? It's just hair, right? I figured as short as I planned to go, bald wouldn't be much of a transition.

About eight months after I cut my hair, I was ready to try being bald. Why I made up my mind in December in Michigan is beyond me, but I wasn't going to let the weather stop me. I decided to let a barber shave me down the first time. I had seen men with razor bumps and I didn't want to deal with adjusting to being bald and having "hair acne" all over my head at the same time.

I was surprised at my apprehension, because to be honest, going bald for me was like a man shaving a 5 o'clock shadow. Not that big of a deal. Seriously.

When I finally got to see my new 'do, I was thrilled! Although the amount of hair cut was equivalent to pencil shavings, there was still a noticeable difference. Bald definitely has its own look.

I walked out of the shop glad that I was back in control. I felt like Cyndi Lauper — it's my hair and I can cut it if I want to. I believe I smiled the whole way back.

Bald was not a style I wore often, as much as I liked it. I did a bald photo shoot and I entered a modeling competition bald, but otherwise, bald was an occasional option, not a permanent hairstyle.

Throughout my life, hair has always been woven in somehow. I am grateful for the ups and downs I experienced as a result of my hair. I didn't enjoy them all, but without them, I wouldn't be the woman I am and would probably still be searching to find myself.

As India.Arie so eloquently expresses, I am not my hair. Despite what society teaches. No matter what others say. In spite of how I'm treated or stared at depending on my hairstyle. I know my worth. I know what I have to offer. With or without hair, I am strong, I am beautiful and I have a purpose to fulfill.

I don't know what the future holds for my hair. I may try locs again; I may not. I might experiment with twists and afro puffs. Or, a bald fade could be how I wear my hair until God calls me home. Either way, I do know that the next time someone says, "It's just hair, right?" I'll smile and say, "Right."

WORKS CITED

[1,3,5,6]*Good Hair*. Dir. Jeff Stilson. Perf. Chris Rock, et al. Lionsgate Home Entertainment, 2010. DVD.

[2,4]Medline Plus (2013). *Sodium hydroxide poisoning*. Retrieved October 14, 2013 from www.nlm.nih.gov/medlineplus/ency/article/002487.htm

[7]National Alopecia Areata Foundation (2013). *About Alopecia Areata*. Retrieved October 2, 2013 from www.naaf.org/site/PageServer?pagename=about_alopecia_intro

[8]National Alopecia Areata Foundation (2013). *Treatment for Alopecia Areata*. Retrieved October 2, 2013 from www.naaf.org/site/PageServer?pagename=about_alopecia_treatment

[9]Simpson, I., Sanders, S., & Ramsey, D. (2005). I am not my hair [Recorded by India.Arie]. On *Testimony Vol. 1, Life & Relationship* [CD]. Atlanta, Georgia: Motown.

NOTES

1951 Laurel Oak Dr.
Flint MI 48507
www.imagepublishings.com

Order Form

Name _____

Address _____

City _____ **State** _____

Zip _____

Qty.	Title	Price	Total
	I Wish I Woulda Knew Me Back Then	**15.00**	
	Coulda Shoulda Woulda	**12.00**	
		Subtotal	$
	Shipping Charges Ground First Book............$3.85 Each additional book..........$1.50	**Shipping** **Total**	$_____ $_____

Make check or money order payable to
Image Publishings

1951 Laurel Oak Dr.
Flint MI 48507
www.imagepublishings.com

Order Form

Name _____

Address _____

City _____ **State** _____

Zip _____

Qty.	Title	Price	Total
	I Wish I Woulda Knew Me Back Then	**15.00**	
	Coulda Shoulda Woulda	**12.00**	
		Subtotal	$
	Shipping Charges Ground First Book.............$3.85 Each additional book..........$1.50	**Shipping** **Total**	$_____ $_____

Make check or money order payable to
Image Publishings

191

www.ingramcontent.com/pod-product-compliance
Lightning Source LLC
Chambersburg PA
CBHW031425250626
47155CB00004B/1631